ethics

activities answer key

bju press®

Greenville, South Carolina

Note: The fact that materials produced by other publishers may be referred to in this volume does not constitute an endorsement of the content or theological position of materials produced by such publishers. Any references and ancillary materials are listed as an aid to the student or the teacher and in an attempt to maintain the accepted academic standards of the publishing industry.

ETHICS Student Activities Answer Key

Writers
Kevin Collins, MDiv
Paul Hornor, MDiv
Bruce Ostrom, PhD

Writer Consultants
Tom Parr, ThM
L. Michelle Rosier

Biblical Worldview
Brian C. Collins, PhD

Academic Integrity
Jeff Heath, EdD

Instructional Design
Rachel Santopietro, MEd
Michael Winningham, MA

Editor
James Zemke, MA

Book Concept and Design
Alayna Rowan

Cover Designer
Emily Rush

Illustrators
Jon Andrews
Jullianna Echardt
Roy Hermelin (Beehive Illustration)
Augusto Zambonato

Production Designer
Sherry McCollough

Permissions
Maria Andersen
Ruth Bartholomew
Sylvia Gass
Hannah Labadorf
Jennifer Walton

Project Coordinators
Allison Brooks
Heather Chisholm

Postproduction Liaison
Peggy Hargis

Photo Credits
Cover Pyrosky/E+ via Getty Images; **39** SDI Productions/E+ via Getty Images; **49** cirano83/iStock/ Getty Images Plus via Getty Images; **55** Ground Picture/Shutterstock.com; **59** 3D_generator/iStock/ Getty Images Plus via Getty Images; **67** michaeljung/Shutterstock.com; **71** fizkes/Shutterstock.com; **77** georgeclerk/E+ via Getty Images

Text acknowledgments appear on-page with text selections.

The text for this book is set in Adobe Minion Pro, Adobe Myriad Pro, Calibri by Monotype, DIN 2014 by Paratype, Free 3 of 9 by Matthew Welch, Freight Macro by Joshua Darden, Freight Sans by Joshua Darden, and Times New Roman PSMT.

© 2024 BJU Press
Greenville, South Carolina 29609

Printed in the United States of America

ISBN 978-1-64626-392-9

15 14 13 12 11 10 9 8 7 6 5 4 3 2 1

contents

using the activities

As you engage with the issues surrounding ethics, you will develop greater aptitude for handling difficult situations with more practice. These activities provide opportunities to practice what you're learning. Many of the activities you do and the skills you hone will be valuable not only for this course but also for life.

ACTIVITIES

The activities will guide you as you engage with each topic. A variety of instructions and questions will help you learn how to carefully apply a Christian ethic.

PRAYER JOURNAL

The prayer journal will help you pray specifically and scripturally based on each lesson's theme.

SCRIPTURE MEMORY

Scripture memory presents key verses related to the lessons. Each Scripture passage includes a brief explanation of the passage's significance.

We can search all over the world for a basis for good and moral living. Throughout history, people have chosen to ground their ethics in the stars, mythological gods, or human reason, among other fallible and finite foundations. Only God is eternal, infinite, omnipotent, omniscient, and omnipresent. God's character is perfect and unchanging and, therefore, is a fundamental foundation for ethics.

THE ATTRIBUTES OF GOD AS A BASIS FOR ETHICS

Choose one of the attributes of God discussed in the Student Edition (holiness, love, goodness, righteousness, trustworthiness) and summarize it below. Explain why it is a key character trait for Christian ethics.

See pages 15–16 of the Student Edition.

_____

_____

_____

_____

Choose one of the following attributes of God not covered in the Student Edition and explain how it impacts Christian ethics.

Truthfulness: *God's truthfulness and inability to lie guarantees that He keeps His promises and follows through on all His pronouncements, whether for blessing or judgment (John 8:26; Heb. 6:18; 1 John 5:20). Therefore, people must be truthful in all their dealings because honesty, sincerity, and truthfulness reflect God's very character (Eph. 4:15, 25).*

Graciousness/mercifulness: *God's gracious character means that He gives and blesses even when the recipients don't deserve it (Rom. 5:8; Eph. 2:7–8). God's merciful character means that He doesn't repay the sinner with quick judgment or judgment at all, even though the sinner was entirely deserving (Psa. 86:15; Titus 3:5). This means that people must reach out to the suffering and the hurting, helping those that are hard to help or difficult to care for. The parable of the Good Samaritan is a tremendous example of a gracious and kind person caring for someone in need (Luke 10:30–37).*

Faithfulness: *God's faithfulness is consistent, unwavering, unbreakable, and everlasting (Deut. 7:9; 1 Thess. 5:24). This means that God always keeps all of His promises and always honors His word. Therefore, people must be faithful in all their dealings with those they must be faithful to. People must keep their word and be loyal to their commitments.*

_____

_____

1.2 Creational Norms and Two Genders

The unbelieving world will fight against God and the order He has established in the universe He created. The fact that God created two genders is seen in Genesis 1–2 and then throughout all of Scripture as well as throughout the created order. Because of this, the creational norm for human genders is that there are just two genders, man and woman.

CREATIONAL NORMS APPLIED TO HUMAN SEXUALITY AND GENDER

Read the article "He Made Them Male and Female: Sex, Gender, and the Image of God" by Christopher Yuan. Describe how the unbelieving world pushes back against God's creational order by trying to establish a new norm for their corrupted views on sexuality and gender.

Example: Today many people reject the gender binary of man and woman, instead recognizing many nonbinary genders.

Those who reject God's creational norm of male and female have exalted themselves and their sins as authoritative. They

are mistaken in their belief that one's sex can be changed and one's gender can be chosen at will. This divergence from

God's clear creational norm is sinful, destructive, and is growing in power and influence.

In your own words, describe the biblical and Christian position of the creational norm regarding human sexuality and gender.

Example: God is the Creator of all and is the absolute authority on all things. Because He created man and woman,

He has established humanity's sexuality and gender. This act of creation was very good (Gen. 1:31) and, as a creational

norm that continued after the Fall, it is good and should be practiced as such. Because of the curse on creation, humans

suffer from all manner of genetic disorders, and some of these are disorders that affect the development of sexual organs.

Nonetheless, these disorders do not disprove the sex binary, and even if they did, they would be the exception that proved

the rule. Disorders of sexual development should not be used to reject the creational norm of two genders, male and female

(Mark 7:21-23; Rom. 1:21-32).

2.1 The Difficulty of Making Ethical Choices in a Fallen World

Making ethical choices can be difficult because of the fallenness of our own hearts, the fallenness of the culture around us, and the fallenness of a world affected by a curse.

Identify an ethical difficulty in each of the following three categories. Relate how the effects of the Fall in each category make ethical decision-making difficult.

THE FALLENNESS OF OUR OWN HEARTS

Examples:

When someone misbehaves, it can be tempting to lie in order to prevent just discipline—a temptation rooted in the sinful human heart. As Christians grow in the virtue of honesty by faith, they will be equipped to resist temptations to bend the truth to their own advantage.

Temptations to participate in self-harm (such as cutting, anorexia, or bulimia) is an unfitting response to anxiety, internal pain, guilt, frustration, anger, or dissatisfaction with body image. As Christians grow in the virtues of self-control and gratitude by faith, they can properly value their bodies and care for them as a gift from God rather than engaging in self-destructive acts.

THE FALLENNESS OF THE CULTURE

Examples:

The common presence of immodest or pornographic images in advertisements, social media, and other media make it very difficult to avoid temptation to lust.

THE EFFECTS OF A SIN-CURSED WORLD

Examples:

Gene therapy and stem cell therapies present promising solutions to the diseases people face because of the effects of the Fall in a sin-cursed world. But these therapies also can be used for unethical purposes, such as creating designer babies, rather than simply fixing an effect of the Fall. These therapies can present difficulties when new stem cells come from "left over" embryos created as part of IVF.

People suffering in extreme ways may be tempted to end their lives through suicide or physician-assisted suicide, and the society around them may also want to be rid of them rather than invest resources to care for them.

2.2 Identifying the Ethical Approaches

Read the following scenarios and identify the approach with one of the following options. Explain your answer.

Deontological Ethics

CONSEQUETIALIST ETHICS
Utilitarian Ethics
Situation Ethics
Ethical Egoism

Virtue Ethics

Existentialism

SCENARIO 1

A health care system is considering allocating the nation's limited medical resources based on a citizen's ability to contribute to the overall welfare of the nation. Providing health care for an individual with no possibility of recovering deprives other citizens of medical attention, and therefore, is not good policy for the majority of citizens. The issue here is not the rationing of limited resources, which would be necessary under any medical system, but the fact that given the limited resources, individuals should be treated based on their ability to contribute to society.

This is an example of operating from a utilitarian ethic. The health care system justifies its actions as doing the greatest good for the greatest number of people, while disregarding the needs and inherent value of those who can no longer contribute to society.

SCENARIO 2

A relative implores you and your family to demonstrate love by happily attending another relative's same-sex wedding ceremony. Many in your family would regard it offensive and unloving if you decided not to attend. The relative argues that a Christian should attend the wedding to show his love for his family member and that his attendance does not equal support for same-sex relationships.

This is an example of situation ethics subjectively defining and applying love.

SCENARIO 3

A guy breaks off a dating relationship because he is not sure he's dating for the right reasons. He is concerned that he is dating just to satisfy some selfish desire for happiness. He says he wants a relationship where he can offer disinterested loyalty without seeking any benefit from the relationship.

This is an example of someone who is operating from a deontological ethic in which disinterested love is seen as the primary duty. He seems to think that he must be loyal, disinterested without seeking any self-benefit, and making decisions without factoring in a desire for personal happiness.

SCENARIO 4

A friend counsels you with this advice: "It's your life. Don't let your parents get in the way of you fulfilling your dreams." You decide to dismiss your parents' concerns about your relationships and choice of college because you are determined to find a partner who makes you happy and attend a college that prepares you for a financially successful career. You plan to do what suits your own desires and plans.

This is an example of ethical egoism because the pragmatic decision to achieve one's end goal is all that matters. (This is not

existentialism because it has more to do with what the person wants to accomplish than it has to do with living out one's

authentic self.)

SCENARIO 5

You've grown up in a fairly sheltered home which followed several traditional social expectations. But now that you have left and are at college, your roommate is opening up a whole new world of possibilities to you—possibilities that were not encouraged or even talked about back home. "You can be anything you want to be! Don't let social conventions hinder you by forcing you into an inferior role. Reject the status quo. Embrace self-care and self-empowerment. Love yourself and be your own greatest hero."

This is an example of existentialism that seeks freedom by throwing off any external constraints to pursue one's own becom-

ing whatever one wishes.

SCENARIO 6

Your classmate is making unintentional mistakes on a project that the two of you are working on together. You need to confront her about these mistakes, but you are nervous about offending her. You decide to begin with a word of appreciation for her help on the project. You then gently point out the areas in the project that need correction by recommending a solution.

This is an example of virtue ethics where you avoid the cowardly response of ignoring the problem and you avoid the unkind

response of harsh criticism. Instead, you act from a courageous and loving character.

Critiquing the
Ethical Approaches

Re-read the scenarios from Activity 2.2 and provide a one- to two-paragraph critique of each one.

SCENARIO 1

Students should address problems with the utilitarian ethic. In this example, the primary problem is that it violates the biblical principle of the sanctity of life for the individual. The greatest good for the greatest number of people takes place at the cost of inequitable treatment of individuals forcibly sectored off into a minority group: those with preexisting conditions. The sanctity of the individual is lost when reasonable provision is taken away by a stilted system. The ends—making insurance cheaper for the majority population and insurance companies more profitable—justifies the means—cutting some people off from medical care or making it an extreme hardship for those who need it most. Students should grapple with whether medical care should be turned into a self-serving moneymaking business endeavor rather than a compassionate service for suffering image-bearers.

SCENARIO 1

Students should address problems with situation ethics. This flawed ethical approach is unhinged from objective, absolute, universal principles. God's commands must define and describe what love is and looks like. Believers who align their lives with God's commands and refuse to celebrate or approve of immoral behaviors and lifestyles are not necessarily being unloving. The most loving thing to do, biblically defined, is to seek an opportunity to lovingly explain why God opposes same-sex lusts and behaviors, then explain the path of repentance God offers from the just punishment for sin. The grace of the gospel always gets offered in the context of a call to repentance. Though Christians face social pressures to accommodate sin, love for God and his glory must be paramount. (Gal. 1:10)

SCENARIO 3

Students should address problems with deontological ethics in which disinterested love is seen as the primary duty. The Bible does not disallow mutual benefit or pursuing happiness that is governed by God's good design and gifts that He wants to bestow upon His creation. This particular ethic has resulted in a misled guilt-trip. The second-guessing, if based only on this concern, is baseless. Certainly, Christians should be seeking God's glory as their ultimate end in any relationship. And they should be seeking to be giving to another for their happiness rather than just selfishly taking for oneself. However, disinterested loyalty is virtually impossible in any relationship. Even God motivates us to love Him because of the good gifts and eternal blessings He has in store for us.

SCENARIO 4

Students should address problems with ethical egoism. A child should follow the biblical principle of honoring his or her parents (which includes obeying them if the child is still under the care of his or her parents). Furthermore, the biblical principles and worldview that parents bring to bear on wise decision-making should not be brushed aside. A young person's plans must be evaluated in accordance with God-honoring goals ad means to achieve those goals. Nonetheless, if parents are not operating according to a biblical worldview, then a child transitioning to adulthood may seek to complete that transition to adulthood by taking full responsibility for him- or herself while still seeking to honor his or her parents even through the disagreement. This person should take great care to make sure his or her plans align with biblical principles rather than being simply pragmatic or selfish.

SCENARIO 5

Students should address problems with existentialism. Status quo social conventions should be evaluated according to biblical principles, creational norms, and the purposes of those human traditions in a culture. The Bible condemns rebellion that seeks freedom from all moral constraints. It also condemns inhospitable and ungrateful behavior that dishonors parents, elders, and other legitimate authorities in a society. Living for self-gratification by any means is a poor end and a self-destructive manner of living.

SCENARIO 6

Students should address problems with virtue ethics. Although it is good to act from a virtuous character, and therefore for you to respond to your classmate with courage and love, we would never know the appropriate circumstances in which to show courage and love without biblical guidance. Furthermore, Christian ethics reminds us that virtuous character is developed in the context of faith in Christ and His Word. Unbelievers may operate according to virtue ethics, but only in a superficial way. True virtue depends on the renewing work of the Holy Spirit in a believer's life.

3.1 Delighting in God's Law

You have learned of the necessity of an objective moral standard for discerning right from wrong. It is one thing to be convinced that God's law is the standard for human behavior; it is another thing to delight in God's law. In reaction to secular society's rejection of biblical morality as outlined in the Ten Commandments, some Christians might misuse the Mosaic law, treating it as an abstract code of ethics for curbing the moral decline of society. But this is not the same as producing changed hearts. For society to conform to God's law, people need to delight in it from the heart. This activity is intended to help you delight in God's law.

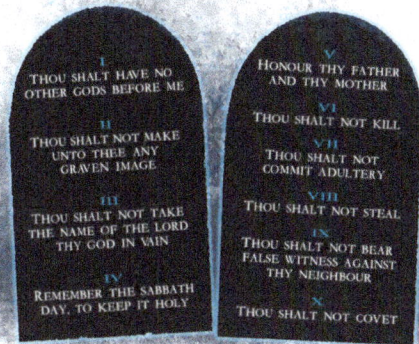

Answer the following questions for the purpose of (1) evaluating your own heart attitude toward God's law and (2) applying the principles of this lesson to influence others to have the right attitude toward God's law.

1. **Even Christians struggle to delight in God's law as they should. Can you think of some reasons for your own struggle in this area?**

   Possible reasons might include the believer's internal conflict between the Spirit and the flesh, neglect of the means of grace, unrepentant sin, a suspicion of God's goodness as it relates to the law, or confusion about the relationship between law and grace.

2. **How might an understanding of God's law as a reflection of God's character increase your delight in His law?**

   When detached from the character of God, the law seems cold and uninviting. Delighting in an abstract code of ethics is difficult but delighting in a person is not. There is much about the person of God and His character that believers find attractive. Seeing God's character in His law makes the law of God appealing to believers.

3. How would you respond to someone who tells you he does not concern himself with the Ten Commandments, but he insists that his ethics leads him to do the loving thing in every situation?

   Response should center on fallen man's inability to know what the loving thing is apart from God's law. Fallen people

   routinely call certain behaviors loving which God calls hateful, and vice-versa.

4. Someone tells you that society is morally bankrupt because it has rejected God's law. She argues that the moral condition of people would improve if the government enforced the Mosaic law. How would you respond to this person?

   A society's law should reflect God's law, and the government should enforce those laws. However, the Mosaic law

   cannot be abstracted from its redemptive historical context. The moral condition of people will never improve apart

   from the redemptive work of Christ. Faith in Christ produces obedience from the heart.

5. What is the relationship between the Ten Commandments and creational norms? How might an understanding of this relationship help you better delight in God' law?

   The Ten Commandments are consistent with creational norms. To break one of the Ten Commandments is to go

   against creation, and that always ends poorly. Delighting in God's law should be enhanced in our lives by the realiza-

   tion that God designed human beings to live one way and not another.

6. Since Christ has fulfilled the Mosaic law on behalf of all who trust Him, what value does the Mosaic law have for Christians?

   While the work of Christ means that the Mosaic law no longer has relevance for Christians as a covenant, the moral

   aspects of the Mosaic law continue to serve as the believer's guide for ethical living.

7. Do you think you would delight in God's law apart from the New Covenant promise of the Holy Spirit? Why?

   No one can delight in God's law apart from the Spirit because all fallen people are in rebellion against God. It takes the

   regenerating work of the Holy Spirit for a sinner to have new affections for God. With those new affections for God

   comes a new delight in God's ways, including His law.

8. **Why is it impossible for a person with the Spirit to be indifferent to God's law?**

   Every person indwelt by the Spirit has God's law written on his heart.

9. **How would you respond to someone who tells you that Christians are not obligated to keep the law because they are no longer under the law?**

   Though Christians are not under the condemnation of the law, their conduct still matters to God. It is inconceivable

   that a Christian could lie, steal, and murder without incurring God's displeasure.

10. **The grammar of the gospel teaches us that the *imperatives* (what we must do as Christians) are made possible because of the *indicatives* (what Christ has done for us). How do you think you would respond to the ethical demands of God's law if Christ had not freed you from its condemnation?**

    Answers may include attempting to escape the condemnation of the law through a strict conformity to its ethical

    demands or replacing the ethical demands of God's law with one that fits a sinful lifestyle.

11. **Christians are called to imitate Christ in holy living, but how can they do this without turning imitation into a self-help strategy for ethical living?**

    Identification with Christ makes imitating Christ possible. Christians who try to imitate Christ without first recogniz-

    ing his or her union with Christ will turn imitation into a self-help strategy for ethical living.

12. **What would you say to a fellow Christian who sees his identity strictly in terms of his failures?**

    The Christian needs to focus on his new identity in Christ. When God looks on His children in Christ, He sees the

    righteousness of Christ, not their failures.

You've learned about the close relationship between wisdom and law and the fact that both are based on creational norms. Becoming a Christian does not automatically make a person wise. To navigate life in this fallen world, believers need to grow in discernment, prudence, and virtue. Recall that wisdom is defined as the art of living well by observing creational norms through the lens of Scripture, by listening to the counsel of the wise, and by being conscious that all of life is lived before the face of God. This activity is intended to help you evaluate competing theories of ethical living based on biblical wisdom as presented in section 3.2.

Read the article "Four Ways to Live More Ethically" by Thomas G. Plante.

1. **Summarize the main points of the article.**

_____

_____

_____

_____

_____

_____

2. **Identify one strength and one weakness of each point from the article based on biblical wisdom as presented in section 3.2.**

_____

_____

_____

_____

_____

_____

3.3 Living for God's Glory

You have learned about the role of motives in making ethical decisions. Why we do is just as important as what we do. In the Christian understanding of ethics, doing the right thing for the wrong reasons does not make an action ethical. A Christian's action is ethical when motived by a desire for God to be glorified in the action. This is the teleology of Christian ethics. While Christians may have additional motives behind their actions, their choices in life should show that God is their greatest delight. This activity is intended to help you live for God's glory.

Answer the following questions to help you evaluate the motives behind your choices and formulate a plan to make God's glory the ultimate motive in your life.

1. **As you think back on a recent ethical decision in your life, what were your motives behind the decision you made?**

   Students should be encouraged to be honest about their motives, even if those motives were not the best of motives.

2. **What questions might you ask yourself to evaluate whether your decision in a particular situation is rightly motivated?**

   Is this choice going to glorify God? Will it make me more like Christ? Will it advance God's kingdom? Will it make me a

   person who is happy in God?

3. **A businesswoman tells you that she financially supports several charitable organizations because it makes her business more profitable. What is your assessment of this person's charitable giving?**

   Though the charitable giving is commendable, the motive for doing so is not.

4. **How can delighting in God help you perform a difficult or undesirable duty?**

   The key to performing any duty is to find some joy in doing it. When the duty itself is difficult or undesirable,

   delighting in God provides the necessary joy that makes the duty easier to perform.

5. **A person chooses to suffer for the sake of Christ rather than enjoy the fleeting pleasures of sin for a season. How does this choice glorify God?**

   It shows that Christ is more desirable than either sin or the absence of suffering.

6. **Living out the Christian ethic in this fallen world can be difficult because the things in this world can be deceptively attractive. How can the values of the kingdom of God help you remain faithful to God when tempted to compromise?**

The believer views the temporary things of this world of little value by comparison to the eternal values of the

kingdom of God. This essential truth helps believers remain faithful.

7. **Jesus motivated His disciples to ethical living by teaching about the amazing blessings that awaited them in the world to come. Do these things motivate you to ethical living? Why?**

Students should be encouraged to answer honestly.

8. **Someone tells you that he thinks Jesus' promise about the meek inheriting the earth is nonsense. His life experience has taught him that those who succeed in this world are the ones who are willing to make ethical compromises. How would you respond to this person?**

Jesus' promise must be received by faith. Those who walk by sight tend to draw the wrong conclusion about who wins

in the end. Some people may experience temporary success by making ethical compromises, but such people will not

inherit the earth.

9. **Jesus promised that the pure in heart will see God. How might this beatitude defend against sexual lust?**

The pleasure of seeing God far exceeds the temporary pleasure of sexual lust. True believers fight for purity of

heart, not because they are trying to earn the privilege of seeing God, but because seeing God is worth the

fighting for purity.

10. **How can God's promise of a glorious future with Him strengthen your resolve as a Christian to live for His glory in this present evil age?**

Living for God's glory in this present evil age can be difficult. Christians are strengthened to live for God's glory by

keeping the glorious future awaiting them in view.

4.1 The Important Place of Virtue in the Bible

Choose one of the virtues listed on the chart below (found on page 65 of your textbook). Complete a Bible study of that virtue, particularly focused on the Wisdom Books in the Bible. Create a presentation on the virtue and what the Bible says about the virtue: definition, description, cultivation and development, and application of the virtue. Your presentation may be a paper, a slide presentation, a blog post, a pamphlet, or other creative idea.

Students may work on this project in conjunction with chapters 5–7. They should be graded based on quality of the content, the presentation, and the grammar.

VIRTUES
faith
love
hope
righteousness
goodness
prudence
diligence
faithfulness
courage
self-control
temperance
patience
humility
meekness
gentleness
kindness
compassion
gratitude
joy
peace
honesty

4.2 Practicing the Spiritual Disciplines

Choose one of the following spiritual disciplines: Bible study, prayer, local church participation, putting sin to death. Request book suggestions from pastors, parents, teachers, or other spiritual mentors on the topic of the spiritual discipline you chose. Read the book (or applicable sections of a book) on that topic. Outline practical ways you can make the spiritual discipline a part of the fabric of your life.

Bible study book suggestion:

Howard G. Hendricks and William D. Hendricks, Living by the Book: The Art and Science of Reading the Bible

(Chicago: Moody Publishers, 2007).

prayer book suggestions:

Donald S. Whitney, Praying the Bible (Wheaton, IL: Crossway, 2015).

D.A. Carson, Praying with Paul: A Call to Spiritual Reformation (Grand Rapids, MI: Baker Academic, 2015), chapter 1.

local church book suggestion:

Wayne A. Mack and Dave Swavely, Life in the Father's House rev. ed. (Phillipsburg, NJ: P&R, 2006).

putting sin to death/sanctification/Christlikeness book suggestions:

Stuart Scott with Zondra Scott, Killing Sin Habits: Conquering Sin with Radical Faith

(Bemidji, MN: Focus Publishing, 2013).

Kris Lundgaard, The Enemy Within: Straight Talk about the Power and Defeat of Sin (Phillipsburg, NJ: P&R, 1998).

5.1 Examining My Faith

Being an ethical person consists of soul-rooted realities, without which it is impossible to manifest the Christian ethic in real-life situations. The virtue of faith is one of these soul-rooted realities. Like an iceberg, the largest chunk of our ethical nature lies beneath the surface of our lives. Therefore, it is vital that we examine ourselves to ascertain the condition of our soul.

Read the following scenarios to assist in your self-examination. Choose two of the four scenarios and write your response.

SCENARIO ONE

Julie is a professing Christian who is very knowledgeable about the Bible, and she serves diligently in her church. She attends all the weekly meetings and is highly respected for her tireless efforts in writing cards to elderly members, working in the nursery, and teaching a women's Bible study. Other church members speak of her as a model Christian, which Julie very much enjoys hearing. She finds her worth and significance in the validation of others rather than in knowing Christ, and she prides herself in her knowledge and service rather than glorifying God for what He has done. Julie is often impatient and critical of other church members who lack her zeal and discipline. She thinks people should be more like her and try harder to be better Christians.

Julie is an example of a person who professes faith but does not possess faith in Christ. Her religious activities spring

from spiritual pride rather than a heartfelt commitment to Christ. She is like the person Jesus described in Matthew

7:22–23. Though she calls Jesus Lord, and though she performs many wonderful deeds, her heart is filled with self-

righteous iniquity. Of the three elements of faith—knowledge, assent, and confidence—the third element is absent

from Julie's life. Despite her busy religious life, Julie has never experienced the joy of trusting Christ.

SCENARIO TWO

Bobby is known at school for his self-confidence, approaching every aspect of life according to the motto "If it's going to be, it's up to me." His self-confidence has grown over the years as his academic success has validated his perception of himself as intellectually superior to others. On the football field, Bobby has distinguished himself as the strongest and fastest athlete on the team. Bobby does not worry about facing challenges too great for him. He is convinced he has the capacity to handle whatever life presents. He regards faith in God as a crutch for weak people who are not strong enough to stand on their own two feet.

Bobby is an example of a person whose faith is misplaced. The object of his faith is himself rather than God. Bobby

wrongly assumes that he has the capacity to handle whatever life presents because he has yet to face a real tragedy

that would test him. The day will come when his strength fails him, causing his self-confidence to crumble. Bobby has

yet to realize that God alone is worthy of a person's absolute confidence.

SCENARIO THREE

Trent considers himself a very spiritual Christian, but he views doctrinal formulations of Christianity to be lifeless and boring. While Trent says that he respects the Bible, he doesn't think knowledge of the Bible is necessary for a robust life of faith. "Reason," he says, "is at odds with faith because faith is like jumping into the unknown." Trent is convinced that his faith is virtuous because it is not limited to what the Bible teaches. He thinks that openness to various spiritual concepts and a preference for ambiguities about the supernatural produces the best kind of ethical behavior.

Trent is an example of someone who separates faith in God from faith in God's Word. His faith is a blind faith based on

his own imagination rather than a knowledgeable faith based on the content of Scripture. He fails to recognize that

faith must be built upon the proper authority of Scripture if faith is to be virtuous. Without an understanding of God's

revelation in Scripture, Trent's faith can neither honor God nor submit to God's will. Therefore, Trent's faith cannot be

virtuous.

SCENARIO FOUR

Sarah is a quiet and unassuming young lady who displays genuine kindness to others. Although her life is filled with difficult and trying circumstances, she exudes a warmth and joy that others attribute to her love for Christ. Sarah is not able to engage in a lot of church activities because of her health problems, but she enjoys reading God's Word and sharing with her friends what God is teaching her. She always seems to be humble in how she discusses the Bible. Because she is aware of the pull of her sinful flesh, Sarah daily depends on the Lord to live an ethical life. Her Christlikeness is evident to all. She trusts that God loves her and that He knows what is best for her life. Therefore, she bases her ethical decisions on the promises of God rather than what she can see with her eyes.

Sarah is an example of a genuine Christian. Her character and life give evidence that her faith is real. All three elements of

faith—knowledge, assent, and confidence—are present in her life. The object of her faith is God rather than herself. She

genuinely values Christ over the things of this world. Her faith is forward-looking; she eagerly waits for God to fulfill His

promises to His people. Her faith is also dependent; she makes regular appeals to God for His enabling grace to respond in

every situation with faithfulness to Him.

You've learned about the direct connection between the things we love and our ethical choices. To be virtuous, we must love that which is good and true as defined by Scripture. What makes love virtuous is not the word itself; many people frequently abuse the word "love" by using vague and empty terms to define it. Evaluate the following video based on a biblical view of love.

Watch the video "5 Definitions of Love" by OWN (Oprah Winfrey Network).

1. Summarize the five definitions of love in the video.

a) "Love is the ultimate truth at the heart of creation" (Deepak Chopra).

b) "Love is acceptance without having to change" (Meagan Good).

c) "Love is life-changing; it teaches us to grow" (Glennon Doyle).

d) Love is always giving what the other person needs (Wintley Phipps).

e) "Love is beyond explanation," and it explains everything good in the world (Maya Angelou).

2. Evaluate each definition based on a biblical view of love.

a) Biblical love cannot be deified. Scripture teaches that God is love (1 John 4:16), but this does not mean that love is God. Love is not "the ultimate truth at the heart of creation"; God is. In addition, human beings are not all the same. Every human being is distinct.

b) Biblical love includes the idea of God accepting us in Christ through faith, but mere acceptance is not love. Biblical love compels us to become more like Christ. That involves change.

c) Biblical love does change our lives, but the speaker offers no specifics. Scripture is very specific.

d) Biblical love is selfless, but not disinterested as the speaker suggests. It flows from seeking one's own happiness in God, which frees believers to love others for the glory of God.

e) Biblical love can be explained, though not exhaustively. While good things can be traced back to God's love, we cannot attribute every good thing to a nebulous concept of love.

OWN. "5 Definitions of Love | SuperSoul Sunday | Oprah Winfrey Network." YouTube video, 2:25. Posted February 13. 2018. https://www.youtube.com/watch?v=qRjTZEkDm18.

5.3 Becoming a More Hopeful Person

You've learned about the necessity of having a well-founded hope. Given the hopelessness in the world today and the various ways that people vainly try to create hope apart from a biblical view of reality, it is essential that Christians nurture their hope in Christ.

The following biblical passages will assist you in your plan for becoming a more hopeful person. Commit to spending a few minutes each day meditating on them.

- Psalm 31:24: "Be of good courage, and he shall strengthen your heart, all ye that hope in the LORD."
- Psalm 42:11: "Why art thou cast down, O my soul? and why art thou disquieted within me? hope thou in God: for I shall yet praise him, who is the health of my countenance, and my God.
- Psalm 119:114: "Thou art my hiding place and my shield: I hope in thy word."
- Psalm 119:116: "Uphold me according unto thy word, that I may live: and let me not be ashamed of my hope."
- Jeremiah 17:7: "Blessed is the man that trusteth in the LORD, and whose hope the LORD is.
- Lamentations 3:24: "The LORD is my portion, saith my soul; therefore will I hope in him."
- Romans 5:3–5: "And not only so, but we glory in tribulations also: knowing that tribulation worketh patience; And patience, experience; and experience, hope: And hope maketh not ashamed; because the love of God is shed abroad in our hearts by the Holy Ghost which is given unto us."
- Romans 8:25: "But if we hope for that we see not, then do we with patience wait for it."
- Romans 15:13: "Now the God of hope fill you with all joy and peace in believing, that ye may abound in hope, through the power of the Holy Ghost."
- 1 Peter 1:3: "Blessed be the God and Father of our Lord Jesus Christ, which according to his abundant mercy hath begotten us again unto a lively hope by the resurrection of Jesus Christ from the dead."

6.1 The Essence of Virtue

While some unbelievers may display outward virtue, they are not what Scripture would call virtuous people. Their virtue is more like the artificial fruit some people showcase on their coffee table. Virtuous people, however, possess genuine spiritual fruit. The former may *display* aspects of virtue, whereas the latter *practice* the essence of virtue.

Answer the following questions to develop this topic.

1. **Based on your understanding of Galatians 5:22–23, do you believe unbelievers can truly possess and practice the virtues listed? Why?**

   This list of virtues is called the "fruit of the Spirit." Therefore, the Spirit is the one who bears this fruit in the lives of those

   He has regenerated and indwells. Unbelievers can't possess the virtues in a deep and real sense because they are neither

   regenerated nor indwelt by the Spirit.

2. **According to Colossians 1:9–10, why can believers bear spiritual fruit and please the Lord with their lives?**

   God is at work in believers' lives. As believers grow in their faith in God, their knowledge, wisdom, and understanding of

   God and His ways grows and deepens. God works in His children's lives, and learning how to practice these virtues is

   part of those good works that believers grow in.

3. **According to 2 Peter 1:3–7, 10, how can people practice these virtues?**

   The calling and election of God energizes believers to do what is righteous and good.

4. **What key phrases from Ephesians 2:10 and Galatians 2:20 undergird the essence of virtue for believers?**

   "created in Christ Jesus"; "Christ liveth in me"; "I live by the faith of the Son of God"

5. The essence of virtue is ___*a God-centered approach to practicing the virtues*___.

   A trying one's hardest

   B avoiding the vices

   C a God-centered approach to practicing the virtues

   D focusing primarily on faith, hope, and love

Any display of virtue by unbelievers doesn't change the fact that they have wrong sources, motives, methods, definitions, and applications of the virtues. Even when they borrow virtues from God's Word and display aspects of virtuous living, unbelievers still lack a holistic God-centered approach to practicing truly virtuous and ethical living.

CLARIFYING TERMS

Write the term that matches the appropriate scenario: "smart," "wise," or "prudent."

_____prudent_____ **1.** Susie always packs a raincoat and an extra change of clothes when she goes hiking with her friends. It often rains spontaneously, making the trails muddy and slippery.

_____smart_____ **2.** Johnny chose the correct answer to the multiple-choice question because he understood the material and figured out the answer accordingly.

_____wise_____ **3.** Dave avoided violence in a fight that broke out at school by tactfully and firmly addressing each party's misunderstandings head-on.

THE APPLICATION TO ABORTION

Prudence is much more than a combination of the appropriate use of knowledge and well-timed wisdom. Consider the topic of abortion. The truth of Scripture is that murder is evil and sinful (Exod. 20:13; 1 Tim. 1:9). Therefore, the murder of any person (unborn, newborn, child, adult, or elderly) is the evil and sinful destruction of an image-bearer of God (Gen. 1:26–27; 9:6).

While pro-life advocates long for the day when abortion is outlawed, different approaches to this goal exist, and success might not guarantee the end of its practice. Some advocates focus primarily on incremental changes in abortion laws, seeking to gain as many limitations on abortion as possible—with the ultimate aim of prohibiting all abortions. Others argue that any law that does not immediately abolish all abortions is an unbiblical compromise. They call for laws to mandate the immediate abolition of abortion.

How might the virtue of prudence guide a Christian with respect to these two approaches to ending abortion?

According to the virtue of prudence, laws that regulate and limit abortion—even if they do not eliminate abortion—

are ethically good as long as they do not hinder the ultimate goal of ending legalized abortion or include other

morally wrong provisions. To demand only the ideal law is imprudent because the result will likely

be continued injustice without progress toward the just end.

Look up and read each passage and summarize its teaching. Then answer the personal application question for each virtue.

Diligence: Colossians 3:17, 23

For the Christian, diligent work and effort involves the recognition of the primary place God has in and over all things.

Gratitude is due to God, who empowers believers to work diligently. Hard work and honest effort reflect a believer's desire to

engage in all undertakings for God's glory.

What is one area of your life where you need greater diligence?

Answers will vary.

Faithfulness: Philippians 3:12–21

Paul was not just diligent in his walk with God. He showed faithfulness by setting aside distractions from God and pursuing

his Savior and Lord. Paul ordered his life in such a way as to wholeheartedly pursue faithfulness to God and His ways.

What is one area of your life which you are struggling to prioritize and be faithful to?

Answers will vary.

Courage: Ephesians 6:10–20

Paul was not scared to obey God by ministering and sharing the gospel. All Christians have the same call to "be strong in

the Lord, and in the power of his might" (v. 10) while following Paul's courageous example to "open my mouth boldly, to

make known the mystery of the gospel" (v. 19). The courage Paul is referencing applies to other areas beyond gospel

proclamation. The gospel's impact and implications lead believers to latch on to the virtue of courage to stand firm in holy

and righteous living. The gospel's impact and implications also embolden believers to speak boldly against unrighteousness

and ungodliness.

What is one area of your life where you habitually lack courage?

Answers will vary.

List some first steps for developing a plan to practice diligence, faithfulness, and courage joyfully and intentionally.

Answers might include the following:

Pray that God would open my eyes to how I fall to the vices of sloth, workaholism, disloyalty, recklessness, and cowardice.

Set up reminders or notifications which prompt me to focus on what needs to get done and limit ways that I waste time.

Set goals for myself regarding diligently getting my work done, staying faithful to the Lord and His Word, and being courageous in my testimony through words and actions.

Shape my life to encourage these virtues by seeking spiritual enrichment from my church through attending the services and youth activities, asking reliable friends to keep me accountable, and serving God in my community whenever I can.

Study the lives of faithful Christians who suffered persecution or martyrdom for taking courageous stands against evil.

6.4 A Dynamic Duo: Self-Control and Temperance

According to the nuance brought out in defining self-control and temperance as we have done in this textbook, the following exercise will help solidify that nuance in practical ways.

Write _A_ if the scenario demonstrates self-control or _B_ if it demonstrates temperance.

_A_ 1. When you and your friends go to a fast-food restaurant, even though they order burgers and fries and you want junk food, you order a salad instead.

_B_ 2. Your friends invite you to go to the mall. Because you've been deliberately using God's Word to strengthen yourself against lust and prepare yourself for temptation, and because you have been virtuous in several recent incidental encounters with lust, you decide to go with them and commit yourself to remain strong against any struggles you might face.

_B_ 3. You have seen the ways that you and others are easily distracted by social media, so you limit yourself to only one social media account and set up a plan to use it responsibly.

_A_ 4. Your coach praises you for your hard work in practice and great performances in games. To avoid asserting yourself over your teammates and to avoid bragging, you choose to not let the coach's praise go to your head.

_A_ 5. Your sibling accidentally ruins one of your favorite outfits. Rather than berating him or her and holding this against your sibling, you recognize how regretful your sibling is and decide to treat him or her with kindness.

_B_ 6. Three months ago, you decided to give up soft drinks. While you struggled with the adjustment initially, today you choose to drink water or juice at restaurants and parties because you now genuinely prefer them to soda.

_A_ 7. While you are on your phone, an ad with inappropriate content starts playing. You immediately block the ad and do what you can to prevent such material from reappearing in the app or browser.

_B_ 8. You have read books and articles on humility and gratitude as a devotional practice. You recognize that pride can easily sneak up on you, and you know what it is like to indulge in and entertain pride. You decide to appreciate humility and gratitude, you enjoy seeing it in others, and you avoid speaking or acting in proud ways.

Imagine a scenario where you lack self-control and therefore struggle to say no to a particular sin. Write a proposal for how you can grow in this virtue.

Students should mention specific Scriptures to read or study as they also focus on practical ways to grow in self-control.

An appeal to one's local church or a mature group of friends for accountability would also be a helpful part of the proposal.

_____

_____

_____

_____

Imagine a scenario where you need to improve in temperance. Write a proposal for how you can grow in this virtue.

Students should mention specific Scriptures to read or study as they also focus on practical ways to grow in temperance.

An appeal to one's local church or a mature group of friends for accountability would also be a helpful part of the proposal.

_____

_____

_____

_____

7.1 Virtues over Vices

Match the correct virtue/vice combination with its corresponding scenario.

> A humility/pride   B meekness/anger   C gentleness/harshness

_C_ **1.** You disagree on various political points and minor issues of theology with certain friends and family members. You are entirely convinced of your positions. You are concerned about their views, which you see as wrong and unhelpful. You love them dearly, but your passion for defending the truth of your beliefs often gets the best of you.

_B_ **2.** Your youth group at church spends time discussing frustrating topics about culture. You find them pointless, a waste of time, and repetitive; you also can't seem to pull your friends out of those discussions while being nice to them. You struggle to keep your cool and not snap at them.

_A_ **3.** You believe that sharing pure facts is an honest and honorable way of reporting information—even if that information is all about you and your successes. You work hard and nothing you have achieved has been given to you. Your home life is challenging, and your parents are by no means wealthy. You crave the satisfaction you feel from sharing your accomplishments or ambitious plans with others.

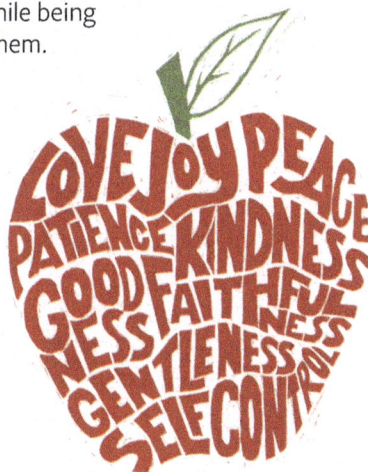

Discuss in groups or list how each of the scenarios above affects your ethical decision-making regarding that specific virtue.

SCENARIO 1

When encountered with contentious issues or topics that good people disagree on, avoid harsh interactions with them by letting gentleness rule in your heart. It is possible to have serious conversations and hold to one's beliefs and positions without being harsh. You can have a good time by being funny and witty without giving up a gentle spirit.

SCENARIO 2

Proverbs 15:1 speaks directly to this situation—"A soft answer turneth away wrath: but grievous words stir up anger." There are any number of ways to practice meekness in this situation. One is to change the topic right away. This usually requires some creativity. The others might realize what you are doing, but they should notice your meekness in doing it, even if they don't agree that they should change the conversation. Avoid getting visibly angry if the frustrating conversation goes on for some time; meekness dictates that you should pull back rather than engage more. Meekly engaging to reprove those in a pointless debate is preferable to getting carried away in an angry rebuke.

SCENARIO 3

Humility and gratitude go hand in hand. When tempted to brag, boast, or say something that undoubtedly will be prideful, thank God for His grace and provision. Humility includes a grateful reliance on God; sharing that reality with others in a self-less way promotes humility and avoids pride. Another way to avoid pride is to always look for ways to humbly compliment others and praise them for how God has worked in their lives. Keep the focus on others rather than yourself.

THE BIBLICAL MODEL OF HELPING THOSE WE CAN

Read the parable of the good Samaritan in Luke 10:25–37. With this biblical account and its teaching on true kindness and compassion in mind, answer the following questions.

1. What was the same in each case when the three men passed by the wounded Jew?

   Each man had the choice to stop, interrupt his plan or trip, interact with a wounded stranger, and give of his time and resources to help him.

2. What other two related virtues (aside from kindness and compassion) are featured in this story?

   love (vv. 27–28) and mercy (v. 37)

3. Why did the Samaritan show kindness to and have compassion on the wounded Jew?

   The Samaritan had developed the virtues of love and mercy. They were part of his character, so those virtues influenced him to show kindness and compassion to this man, despite the complicated history surrounding their ethnic differences.

4. Who are your neighbors that God calls you to love?

   Everyone I interact with.

5. Describe a circumstance where you would show kindness to someone with whom you normally wouldn't interact.

   Answers should include expressing kind words and actions to classmates that aren't friends, others rejected by one's peers or society in general, the elderly, those with disabilities, or anyone that isn't a direct peer. Kind words would include congratulating someone, complimenting them, greeting them kindly, or inquiring about their well-being. Kind actions would include inviting that person to eat at one's table, joining their team, helping them with something, or offering to pay for a meal.

6. **Describe a circumstance where you would show compassion to someone with whom you normally wouldn't interact.**

   Answers will be similar to the answer to the question above. Compassion is stirred in one's heart because one sees the

   difficult circumstances or injustices someone else is experiencing. These examples would likely require one to give more

   of one's time and resources to help meet someone's need. Examples might include helping a friend get counseling they

   need, supporting them as they meet with a pastor or counselor, raising funds and giving of one's own funds to help

   someone in dire need.

A MODERN-DAY LESSON IN HELPING THOSE WE CAN

The situation in the Xinjiang region of China is dire. For many decades the Chinese minorities who live there, especially the Muslim Uyghurs, have suffered persecution from the Chinese government, and since 2016 the genocidal program against the Uyghur people has only gotten worse. What is threatened is the Uyghur identity, culture, language, dress, religion, health, freedom, and lives. Han Chinese, the majority people group in China, are being sent to Xinjiang to forcibly live with Uyghur families to keep tabs on them and be a Chinese majority influence on them. At least one million Uyghurs have been imprisoned for various "crimes" against the state. Forced sterilizations of women and forced labor are also common. In recent years, China has accelerated its once gradual mission to force the Uyghur people to assimilate into main Chinese culture and, sadly, that mission includes genocide. While the Chinese government denies all allegations, these are real crimes against humanity occurring in our day.

Listen to Part 3 of the January 19, 2022 episode of *The Briefing* by Al Mohler (starting at 14:47) and evaluate the ethics of the situation.

There is no need to feel guilty about not being able to help those whom you can't help. You might desire to help a people group or an individual suffering persecution, but you don't have access to them. That is good and righteous. But because you have limitations, you can't do all that you might want to do to show compassion to hurting people. However, there are those who can do something and should.

1. **Given the situation of the Uyghur people and the comments made by Chamath Palihapitiya, what ethical choices are facing the NBA?**

   The NBA is responsible for business dealings directly with China. Any pressure by the NBA on China for their treatment

   of the Uyghur people will most likely result in lost revenue to the NBA. Billions of dollars are at stake, so the NBA casts

   a blind eye to the unethical treatment of the Uyghurs by the Chinese government.

2. **How has Chamath Palihapitiya made an unethical choice?**

Chamath Palihapitiya readily admits to supporting his investment in an NBA team over helping a suffering people.

The value of human life—of image-bearers of God—always trumps financial gain or public image. Willingly and

publicly closing one's eyes to the dire situation is the epitome of an unethical position.

3. **What ethical approach are the NBA and Chamath Palihapitiya subscribing to by ignoring the plight of the Uyghur people and failing to show them kindness and compassion?**

the consequentialist approach

4. **How should kindness and compassion shape the responses of each person involved in the situation?**

The well-being of suffering people motivates both kindness and compassion. When the oppressor is powerful and

influential, the methods to effect change have to be serious. Kindness must shape the response of those involved.

Compassion must shape the response of them to do what it takes to meet the needs of the suffering people. Love for

God and love for others makes room for this kindness and compassion. These virtues, along with the others

necessary to achieve the goal, should shape each response of every person involved.

5. **What ethical choices face fans of the Golden State Warriors or of the NBA?**

Fans of the NBA and the Golden State Warriors have to justify their participation in this severe lack of kindness and

compassion for a persecuted people group based on the extent to which they support the NBA and the Golden State

Warriors. We aren't responsible for the free and voluntary actions of others. But, knowing the details of this situation,

believers have the responsibility to display the virtues of kindness and compassion. This is right, even if the kindness

and compassion take place indirectly or from a distance and don't seem to have direct impact on the basketball

league or the Uyghurs.

6. Even though you aren't able to influence China to stop persecuting the Uyghur people, you can apply these principles to exercising kindness and compassion in your community. What ways could you endeavor to apply these principles by showing kindness and compassion in your community?

Prudently decide what fundraisers of community groups or organizations are worth participating in. Search out and support community outreaches that reach those who are down and out. Rely on various virtues to discern which programs are harmonious with the gospel and have a trusted track record of turning around the lives of those individuals. Inquire at my own church or another church in the area to see if they already partner with an organization like this.

7.3 The Vice of Worry

Answer the following questions.

1. **What sort of behavior results from excessive worrying?**

   Answers may include fretting over small things, unease when a situation is unresolved, or imagining multiple

   scenarios where things go wrong.

2. **What excuses are commonly given to justify excessive worrying?**

   Answers may include genuine concern for one's safety and well-being, desire to show love and appreciation for

   someone, great interest in something yet to come, or a lack of knowledge about something.

The vice of worrying is related to anxiety, which is made up of uneasiness and fear. Believers should not be characterized by worry or anxiety. Peace is the virtue that the Spirit develops in the lives of believers, and that peace snuffs out worry.

Read 2 Corinthians 4:7–16. Answer the following questions based on this passage.

1. **What virtues are referenced either explicitly or implicitly in this text?**

   7: *humility*

   8: *peace*

   9: *faithfulness*

   13: *faith*

   14: *hope*

   15: *gratitude*

   16: *patience*

2. **Does this passage leave any room for the vice of worry to be part of a Christian's practice? Explain your answer.**

   No. Because believers have the life of Jesus in them spiritually, they can have peace despite any physical troubles or

   harm. Spiritual life and a resurrection to eternal life awaits those that die in the Lord. God gets the glory for the daily

   renewal of His children, even when they experience challenging circumstances.

3. **What challenges are you facing today where you find yourself tempted to give in to the vice of worry rather than to the virtue of peace?**

   Answers should include how peace offers a solution to those challenges that produce worry. Look also for reference

   to the other virtues in this section (gratitude and joy), as well as those mentioned in the passage above.

Describe how practicing the virtue of peace enables you to ethically manage the following situations.

SCENARIO ONE

A good friend has expressed serious doubts about her faith in the Bible as God's Word and in Jesus as a sufficient Savior.

She can have peace in knowing that the trustworthiness of God's Word and the faithfulness of Jesus as Savior can't be

diminished or overturned by anyone or anything. These realities remain true regardless of who believes in them or not. She

can have peace in knowing that God is at work in her life. You can calmly and in faith try to point her to truth. She can rest

peacefully that God is at work and can be trusted.

SCENARIO TWO

Someone in your immediate family has received a life-threatening diagnosis.

You can have peace by trusting in the God who is sovereign over even the sicknesses and illnesses that plague all people.

Though facing death is difficult and challenging, you can experience and share God's peace by trusting in God and making

the most of a hard situation.

SCENARIO THREE

You are anxious about finishing high school with good grades, taking college entry exams, and getting into the college you want.

Part of practicing the virtue of peace is preparing as well as you can for each quiz, test, and exam. This doesn't mean you

must perfectly or ideally prepare, but you should faithfully do your best. You can have peace that this is what God

expects from you. The Lord ultimately determines what colleges accept your application, so you can have peace by resting in

God for that answer.

SCENARIO FOUR

Your friend group is going through some changes as people start dating or finding other interests.

Though some of these changes might be unsettling to you, you can have peace in knowing that you will do what you know

to be best. In the face of pressure, direct or indirect, you can be at peace in knowing that these social changes don't have to

affect you in a significant way. You can have peace while trusting the Lord to give you grace as you navigate the changing

social landscape of your friend group.

7.4 Don't Tell Yourself Lies

Did you realize that the virtue of honesty includes telling yourself truths rather than lies?

To believe a lie is to tell yourself an untruth, which is harmful to your thinking, decision-making, and living. The pursuit of honesty includes not only speaking the truth and being honest in all your dealings but also guarding against telling yourself lies.

Use the following questions to create a personal environment that is hospitable to the virtue of honesty and inhospitable to the vices of lying and falsehood, even when you entertain them in your mind and embrace them in your heart.

1. **What are some common lies that people your age are likely to believe?**

   Answers may include that social acceptance, being attractive, or having success will bring happiness; being young means you don't have to be responsible or disciplined; or that young people should have a large impact on the world; or that young people can't contribute anything valuable to society.

2. **How would you correct these lies with the truth?**

   Acceptance from other people is a natural desire for all people, but God hasn't set that as the requirement for joy or happiness. God has given all believers acceptance through Christ and gives varying levels of love and support from loved ones and other believers (Eph. 4:15–16, 31–32).

   Physical attractiveness is subjective. Its standards are constantly changing, and it isn't an indicator of anything worthwhile to God (Prov. 31:30; Matt. 23:27). In God's economy, character is far more valuable than good looks (1 Pet. 3:4).

   Success is not a guarantee in life. Faithfulness is what God requires of His children (Matt. 25:14–27). Christians need to believe the truth that doing the best they can with what God has given them provides actual satisfaction.

   God can use all people of all ages. He even used a donkey once to teach a man a lesson (Num. 22:22–35). Children or young people are found in Scripture doing great (David versus Goliath in 1 Samuel 17; Naaman's servant girl in 2 Kings 5:1–14) and practical (boy who offered his lunch for the feeding of the five thousand in John 6:9–11) things for God.

   Ethical living applies to all Christians, and youth or immaturity is not an excuse for unethical decisions or lifestyles. Everyone requires time to mature in all areas of life. Christ commands His followers to obey His commands, regardless of age (John 14:15). Believers need to carefully guard against distractions that would hinder their walk with the Lord.

Write a paragraph explaining how believing a specific lie has harmed you. Include how understanding the biblical correction will benefit you moving forward.

_____

_____

_____

_____

_____

_____

_____

_____

_____

_____

_____

8.1 The Components for Making Ethical Decisions

Create a pamphlet, blog, slideshow, or other form of presentation that overviews Acts, Agents, Ends, and Context. Use that tool to present this information to someone outside your class. Ask that person or group to respond to the following questions.

1. List three insights into this biblical approach to ethics that you found helpful.

2. Identify two effects that you think this approach would have if more people followed it.

3. What is one question that you still have about this approach?

Choose two of the following topics. Write a test case for each of them regarding a hypothetical scenario that requires an ethical response. Discuss your test cases with a classmate or with the entire class. Be prepared to rightly answer the four main questions from the practical method for ethical decision-making.

Topics

- Abortion
- Addictive substances or habits (like gambling)
- Civil disobedience
- Environmentalism
- Illegal immigration
- Making use of medical science (like organ donation)
- Racial discrimination
- Self-defense
- Sexual purity
- Social media use and other media use
- Suicide
- Work ethic

Four Main Questions

- Context: What is the context of this ethical decision?
- Acts: What does the Bible say about this issue, and what creational norms reflect God's design?
- Ends: What sorts of outcomes might various decisions in this situation lead to?
- Agents: What motivations are involved—what virtues are exhibited and what vices are avoided?

9.1 Unethical Killings

Formulate a biblical response to the following scenarios.

SCENARIO ONE

A drunk driver kills a loved one.

There is a biblical place for righteous anger that calls for justice. Demanding that the authorities charge the drunk driver with murder may seem appropriate, but in legal terms, the driver's initial crime was driving under the influence of alcohol, and the death of the loved one was the unintended result of this lesser crime. Therefore, the proper biblical response to this form of unethical killing is for the drunk driver to be charged and convicted of involuntary manslaughter.

SCENARIO TWO

A heated argument between two neighbors turns violent, with one neighbor striking the other in the face with sufficient force to kill him.

While the first neighbor did not intend to kill the second neighbor, he is still responsible for the death. The use of physical force in a heated situation means that the first neighbor is held to greater legal accountability than would apply with involuntary manslaughter. His actions were intended to cause harm, albeit not death. Therefore, the proper biblical response is for the first neighbor to be charged and convicted with voluntary manslaughter.

SCENARIO THREE

A vicious dog's owners carelessly allow it to run free in the neighborhood until one day the dog attacks and kills a child.

The owners of the dog are responsible for the child's death because they knew the dog was vicious, and they should have known that the dog needed to be restrained and prevented from running free in the neighborhood. The fact that they did not intend the child's death does not exonerate them. Because of their carelessness, the owners of the dog should be charged and convicted with involuntary manslaughter.

SCENARIO FOUR

After an elderly woman passes away in a nursing home, it is found out that a nurse spent weeks enacting a plan to be written into the woman's will before intentionally administering her a lethal dose of drugs.

The nurse not only intentionally killed the elderly woman, but she did so with premeditation and for the purpose of deceptively stealing her money. This form of unethical killing fits the description of first-degree murder. A biblical response would require that the nurse face either the death penalty or life imprisonment.

9.2 Counsel for Suicide and Euthanasia

Research a biblical counseling resource (book, chapter in a book, booklet, journal or magazine article, blog, sermon, or other media) on suicide and/or euthanasia. Focus on the advice the resource provides on how to respond to someone who has experienced the loss of a loved one to suicide or euthanasia. Suggested resources can be found at biblical counseling websites like CCEF (Christian Counseling and Educational Foundation) or ACBC (Association of Certified Biblical Counselors).

Write a sample dialog of how you would respond to a friend who has experienced such a loss based on the advice you gleaned.

_____

_____

_____

_____

_____

_____

_____

_____

_____

_____

_____

_____

_____

_____

_____

_____

_____

_____

_____

_____

9.3 About Abortion

Work with a classmate to create a helpful pamphlet you can share with friends. Create an inviting design that answers common questions and discusses scriptural concerns. Select from the questions below or create one for the group.

How do you begin a conversation with someone who may intend to have an abortion?

How do you relate the gospel to someone's practical struggles that have led them to consider or to go through with an abortion?

How can I talk to a friend who is considering or who has already had an abortion?

What should I do if a friend is going to secretly get an abortion?

How can you show compassion without compromising the truth when talking with someone being pressured to get an abortion?

How do you persuade and help someone keep the baby, even when difficult circumstances and others' recommendations suggest otherwise?

You will find that people hold various positions on capital punishment. Not everyone you encounter will be equally knowledgeable about why they believe what they believe. How can you best respond to those who have an incorrect view about the justice of the death penalty?

Answer the questions to develop your understanding of the biblically warranted legitimacy of capital punishment.

1. **Why does Jesus' teaching about "turning the other cheek" not invalidate the death penalty in murder cases (Matt. 5:38–39)?**

   Jesus was addressing personal retaliation or retribution, not the punishment of murder.

2. **If God doesn't get any pleasure from the death of the wicked (Eze. 33:11), how could He have also mandated the death penalty (Gen. 9:5–6)?**

   In Ezekiel the context shows that God is lamenting that Judah (and Jerusalem specifically) will be punished for its sinful idolatry and rebellion. This passage aligns with the "life for life" teaching in Genesis because their wicked deeds are justly punished. There is forgiveness for the sin of murder, but it is just to follow through with that sin's consequences.

3. **If God and the family of the murder victim forgive a repentant murderer, would it be just for the recently converted murderer to be spared from the death penalty?**

   Though the converted murderer has been forgiven and will not be eternally punished for his sin, he is still responsible to the law for his crime. Scripture does not remove the consequences of criminal behavior simply because the criminal is repentant. True repentance includes accepting the just punishment that is due within society. A society that automatically spared repentant murderers from the death penalty would encourage rampant false repentance.

For many Christians who serve in the military, it is an honor to serve their country in this way. Serving stateside or fulfilling an assignment in a foreign land outside of wartime is very different from personally going to war and serving in combat. The ethical issue of fighting a just war and doing so justly only arises when one actively participates in a war.

Answer the following questions to assess what considerations are necessary if one is called upon to fight in a war.

1. How would you assess the ethical nature of the war you are being called upon to fight in?

   Answers should include a reference to the tenets of just war doctrine on page 174.

2. One's responsibility before God is greater than one's responsibility to one's job or one's country. How would you approach your responsibilities if the war you are suddenly involved in is unjust?

   Answers might include a conversation with one's superior officer to be exempt from participating in at least direct involvement in any frontline combat; a request to transfer to a position in the military that isn't directly involved in the war; or resigning from one's role or job in the military.

3. How would you deal with potential pushback from coworkers, friends, or family who criticized your decision to avoid participating in an unjust war?

   This must be done with grace and patience. Suffering the consequences of a right decision, though unpopular, isn't anything new for Christians of any age. The criticism one might encounter could be an open door to share one's careful and ethical approach to war. Much prayer should accompany this whole process and its potential fallout. God sustains the righteous who suffer for the sake of truth (1 Pet. 3:13–17).

Use the following three steps to begin to formulate an ethical approach to reforming the current immigration policy in the United States.

1. Research the current statistics on immigration (legal and illegal), looking at the costs and benefits of legal immigration as well as current trends surrounding illegal immigration (where it is happening the most and what is driving it). Offer suggestions to reduce illegal immigration. Be sure to look at sources from a variety of perspectives.

2. Research proposed solutions to the problem of illegal immigration. Evaluate whether they are realistic, effective, and moral.

3. Research ways immigrants are shown compassion and generosity. Evaluate these ways in light of the biblical virtues of prudence, righteousness, and compassion. Balance the real needs many immigrants have with the importance of obeying the law.

Consult pages 182–83 for application of the three virtues.

In groups, or individually, list issues that would require disobedience to civil authority if they were made into laws.

Answers may include denial of the faith or Christ, affirmation of a heretical teaching, proclaiming blasphemy, a denial of

God's creation of two genders and His plan for marriage, or disobeying or supporting disobedience of the Bible.

In groups, or individually, read the following scenarios and provide a response that would promote an ethical disobedience of authority. Include the relevant Scriptures that you would use in support of the ethical disobedience.

SCENARIO 1

A Christian joins a small house church, despite living in a country where house churches are considered illegal. During a worship service, the police interrupt the meeting and the Christian is detained. The totalitarian and religiously oppressive government offers him freedom if he forsakes his faith in Christ. If he does not forsake his faith in Christ and the Bible, he will remain imprisoned in harsh conditions for an undetermined amount of time. Why is it ethical for him to refuse to affirm what the government requires of its citizens?

This government clearly requires the Christian to deny his or her faith (Ps. 14:1). Loving and obeying God supersedes any

human institution's commands to the contrary (Matt. 22:36–40). Believers are to worship God not only in the privacy of their

own minds, but also in spirit and in truth (John 4:24). Doing so will be evident to others. Remaining faithful to God is pos-

sible because of God's sustaining grace, even in persecution that results from disobeying a tyrannical limitation on religious

freedom (John 16:33; 1 Pet. 3:14–17).

SCENARIO 2

The government passes a law prohibiting any non-homeschool educational entity (public, private, Christian, etc.) from teaching creationism. What should Christian schools do? What should Christian parents do?

Christian disobedience to this law is ethical not only because the Christian teacher is bound to teach God's truth (Acts 5:29),

but also because such violation of the law would likely be part of the expected legal challenge. Christian parents will need to

consider their options, including being informed about what their children's schools will do. Homeschool could be an option

for many. In the American legal context, with the presence of the first amendment, such a law would likely be quickly struck

down as unconstitutional.

11.1 Responding to Racism with Grace and Truth

Formulate a biblically wise response to the following scenarios using the given Scripture passages:

1. **A friend uses a racial slur in your presence (Ps. 109:2–3; Prov. 10:18).**

   Pray before speaking to your friend so you can communicate in the best way possible. Perhaps you could ask your friend how he would feel if someone used a racial slur to describe him. If your friend becomes defensive, you may simply ask him not to use racial slurs in your presence because you don't like when God's image-bearers are dehumanized.

2. **A family member is dismissive about the enduring impact of slavery in America (Job 30:25; Rom. 12:15–16).**

   Acknowledge that conditions in America have greatly improved for African Americans, and for this we can and should be grateful to the Lord. Then ask your family member if he thinks that there is room for more improvement regarding race relations in America. If your family member agrees, then ask him if it might improve race relations if the majority of people were more sympathetic toward African Americans who have experienced racial discrimination. Admitting this point does not require one to embrace the "white responsibility" solution to race relations in America.

3. **A teacher discusses the issue of voter identification, and a student in your class asserts that voter identification laws are motivated by racism (Prov. 18:13).**

   Ask your fellow classmate if she could give you evidence that voter identification laws are motivated by racism. If she provides legitimate evidence, you might state that while some people intend to suppress voter turnout among minorities with voter identification laws, many people simply intend for the law to keep elections fair and honest. Then ask if the teacher could provide any statistics in support of voter identification laws among African Americans. If support for voter identification laws is reasonably high among African Americans, ask the fellow classmate why any African American would support a law that is motivated by racial animus toward them.

4. **A guest preacher is invited to speak to your majority white congregation to promote racial harmony. His message centers on calling the white church members to repent of their "white privilege" (Eph. 2:13–18).**

   We can acknowledge the historical sins against black Americans and the fact that many whites have had advantages that many blacks have not, but not all white Americans are complicit in these historical sins. Those who are born white have not sinned by being born into a family of privilege. Many people of minority groups today are also born into privilege. Therefore, "white privilege" is not a sin for which white Americans need to repent. The church is united in Jesus Christ, and the message needed for racial harmony is one that calls believers to treat ethnically diverse believers in a manner consistent with their existing unity as members of the body of Christ.

Consult a resource (journal or magazine article, blog, sermon, or other media) on substance abuse or gambling.

Suggested articles:

"Is Marijuana as Safe as We Think?" by Malcolm Gladwell
"Seven Reasons Not to Play the Lottery" by John Piper
"How Casinos Enable Gambling Addicts" by John Rosengren

Additional resources can be found at websites like the Ethics and Religious Liberty Commission (ERLC).

Write a sample dialog of how you would respond to someone pressuring you to engage in one of these vices based on the advice gleaned from the resources that you consulted. You should think through common objections, questions, or pushback that you could face in such a dialog, and then respond in a biblical manner.

_____

_____

_____

_____

_____

_____

_____

_____

_____

_____

_____

_____

_____

_____

_____

_____

_____

_____

_____

_____

_____

11.3 Ethical Challenges with Social Media

Formulate a biblically wise response to the following scenarios using the given Scripture passages.

1. How might you resist the temptation to compare your life with people on social media? Do you think the lives you see on social media are carefully curated, and how might that change the way you see your life? (2 Cor. 10:12)

   Knowing who you are in Christ and finding contentment in the Lord and with the life He has given you is essential for resisting the temptation to compare your life with others. Besides, most people's lives are completely different from how they appear on social media. We don't see a person's troubles and difficulties on social media. You might use this knowledge to be more mindful of the blessings in your own life.

2. What would be a compassionate response to someone who has been bullied on social media? (Matt. 10:31)

   Reassure the person of how much people care for her and encourage her to counter the lies of the bullies with the truth of God's Word. Her worth is not determined by cruel comments posted on social media. Instead, God's Word tells her that she is more valuable to God than the birds of the air.

3. What would be an unbiblical response to a person who posted on Twitter a political view with which you strongly disagree? How might you respond to the post with wisdom? (Titus 3:1–2)

   An example of an unbiblical response would be to post a snide comment, denigrating the individual. A wise response would be to post a thoughtful and respectful post, offering a clear reason for your disagreement.

4. How might you make use of social media to be a faithful representative of Jesus Christ? (Prov. 12:17–23)

   Stop and think twice before posting on social media. Make sure the substance and tone of your comments are in keeping with the biblical virtues. Guard your heart and mind by avoiding inappropriate forms of social media.

5. Who could you talk to if you have experienced bullying on social media?

   You could talk to a parent, a pastor, a Bible teacher, or another godly adult. Students may consult one of these people and summarize the advice they received.

11.4 Business Ethics

Interview a business owner and/or someone who leads a company and who frequently makes difficult decisions to ensure the success of the business without compromising biblical ethics. Select from the questions below and/or add some of your own.

What ethical qualities do you look for when hiring a new employee?

What has been the most difficult ethical decision you have had to make in your position?

How do you balance maximizing business profits with the biblical warnings against the love of money?

Are you aware of any legal yet unethical business practices that give your competitors an edge in the marketplace, and how have you convinced your company to avoid such practices?

What steps do you take to ensure that you are setting a Christlike example for your employees with respect to your work ethic?

What methods do you use to motivate your employees to perform their jobs, and are there certain methods you avoid because they are not consistent with a biblical ethic?

Record a brief video articulating three things you learned and three personal applications.

12.1 Editing the Human Germline

To edit the human germline means to permanently alter the way someone exists on a cellular level. This change would affect any descendants that a person might have. Human gene editing is irreversible. Little is known about the effects on the individual or on the individual's descendants.

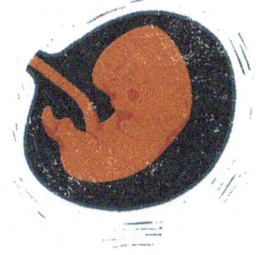

Read the article "Should we edit the human germline?" by Jon Heggie. Write a biblical response to the author's arguments for and against editing the human germline. Weigh the costs and benefits of each and then reach a conclusion.

Responses to Arguments for Human Germline Editing

Immediacy: *Gene mutations cause serious diseases. Human germline editing offers a solution to this specific result of the Fall that impacts hundreds of thousands of individuals and their families around the world. The fact that Jesus healed individuals with serious diseases during His earthly ministry proves that God is not against treatment of genetic diseases.*

Permanence: *The challenge of trying to eradicate the genes responsible for a serious disease is that there may be an unknown impact on other genes and on subsequent generations. Our decisions today must be ethical, so we must consider the outcomes that could happen twenty or forty years from now. The biblical principle of being kind and loving to one another, including not harming one another, applies to those in the present as well as to those who will be born in the future (Matt. 22:39).*

Regulation: *Government regulation that aligns with the ethical concerns of this issue should be welcomed (Rom. 13:3–4; 1 Pet. 2:14). Medical science affects many people in a big way, so it is tragic when anyone abuses scientific advances, especially those people in positions of power.*

Progress: *Vaccinations, antibiotics, and antiviral medications are ethical and comparatively recent scientific advances. Human germline editing currently appears to be the next step. Believers should know that progress for progress's sake cannot be justified biblically (1 Cor. 10:31).*

Certainty: *Even though the option exists to screen babies in the womb and use human germline editing to avoid a debilitating or life-threatening condition, it is full of risk. There may also be societal pressure to abort babies that can't be "fixed." It is not prudent to go forward with something where the risks outweigh the ethically questionable benefits (Prov. 16:1–5).*

Responses to Arguments against Human Germline Editing

Consent: *It isn't loving to perform life-altering procedures on individuals without their permission, even if with good intentions and results. If there were no risk involved and an absolute guarantee that the procedure would be successful, then the topic of consent would be much less of an issue. God is sovereign and has a plan for every individual's life; it is not in the hands of people to determine this for others. Doing unto others as we would want them to do unto us applies in this case (Matt. 7:12).*

Uncertainty: *Wisdom and adequate preparation are needed prior to doing something as impactful as human germline editing (Luke 14:28–30). It takes humility to recognize the restraints and limitations that we have. There is still great uncertainty regarding the success rate of human germline editing and what the ramifications are for that individual and any future descendants.*

Permanence: *The irreversible nature of human germline editing should give many people pause and prompt great care in research and decisions. The widespread and long-term effects are also two crucial factors. No one knows the side effects of eradicating certain mutations or genetic effects from localized or global populations, and it is unknown what influence this could have on the rest of society. Unprecedented scenarios with this level of impact are a cause for much wisdom and prudence (Prov. 3:5–7).*

Eugenics: *There is a real danger of editing the human genome to the extent that certain features can be added or removed from human embryos so "designer babies" can be created. This is an application of human germline editing that is for looks, not for health. The options could include eye color, height, muscular build, and intelligence. All these are traits that parents would likely want to determine so their children have advantages over their peers. This application is not medicine in the true sense of the word; it is a mere demonstration of the scientific and medical capabilities. God warns against trying to be smarter or wiser than He is (Ecc. 7:15–19).*

Social: *If human germline editing became widespread, only the rich would have access to it. This reality would compound an already divided and disunified society as the rich would develop children and future generations with unique advantages or supposed improvements. It's possible that these individuals would be more respected and be looked upon as great influencers on the rest of society, which may create animosity between groups and strain relationships. Christians should fight against the sin of showing partiality (James 2:1–4). While hypotheticals do not make for strong ethical arguments, human germline editing has the potential to make this type of partiality in society even worse.*

Adapted from:
Heggie, John. "Should we edit the human germline?" Published December 17, 2018. https://www.nationalgeographic.com/science/article/partner-content-genom-editing

12.2 Paying for Organ Donations?

While considered an impossibility one hundred years ago, organ transplants are now common practices in hospitals, with thousands of procedures performed each year. In many places in the world, these transplants rely on a donation system, in which the donors freely volunteer their organs for this purpose and expect nothing in return. However, there are those who say individuals or their families should be paid for the organs they supply. The idea is that this kind of scenario is a win-win. However, this proposition raises serious ethical questions.

Answer the questions below to develop a biblical response to the practice of paying people for organ donations.

1. **What is the difference between buying an item from a shopping center and buying someone's organs?**

   Organs are part of peoples' bodies and therefore part of who they are as people. A purchasable item at a store is a commodity unless it is food or water. The human body should not be commodified. The difference between the two examples is categorical.

2. **What does the Bible say about our bodies?**

   God fashioned man and woman in His image (Gen. 1:26–27; 2:7, 22). Our bodies are part of God's image and should therefore be treated with respect and dignity. Believers in particular should surrender their bodies to God out of gratitude and worship (Rom. 12:1; 1 Cor. 6:19–20). To take someone's life in the purchase of an organ needed for life is to disrespect God because people are made in His image (Gen. 9:6). Even if a life isn't lost through the purchase of an organ for transplantation, our bodies aren't items for sale to the highest bidder. This approach is also offensive to the image of God in man.

3. **What does the Bible say about how we are to treat one another?**

   To treat someone with the dignity and respect they deserve is to love them as we naturally love ourselves and our own wellbeing (Matt. 7:12; 22:39). Some might be tempted to purchase an organ illegally and unethically to save the life of a family member. However, if someone were pressured to sell an organ of a sick or dying loved one, there would undoubtedly be opposition to such an unethical approach even in the face of extreme circumstances.

4. **Why is it offensive and degrading to attempt to buy or sell human organs rather than relying on a system of organ donation?**

   Though people can pay enough money to the right person to get about anything in the world, that mere fact doesn't

   make doing so just or righteous. People are more than a collection of their organs. Humans are the union of their

   material and immaterial parts. It is offensive and degrading to treat a person as a mere collection of organs and

   tissues and bones.

5. **What does considering paying someone to obtain an organ for transplantation communicate about one's trust in a sovereign God?**

   Unethical and sinful things do not conform to God's character. No matter how extreme the circumstance,

   the sin of objectifying fellow image bearers to unethically extract their organs to save the life of another

   image-bearer doesn't demonstrate trust in God's sovereignty. Buying or selling someone's organs goes against

   a sense of gratitude to God and worship of Him for sovereignly making each person according to

   His design. Failed organs are part of a fallen world, but God can still accomplish His purposes, and He has

   established laws and boundaries to define immoral behavior.

Mishandling Creation

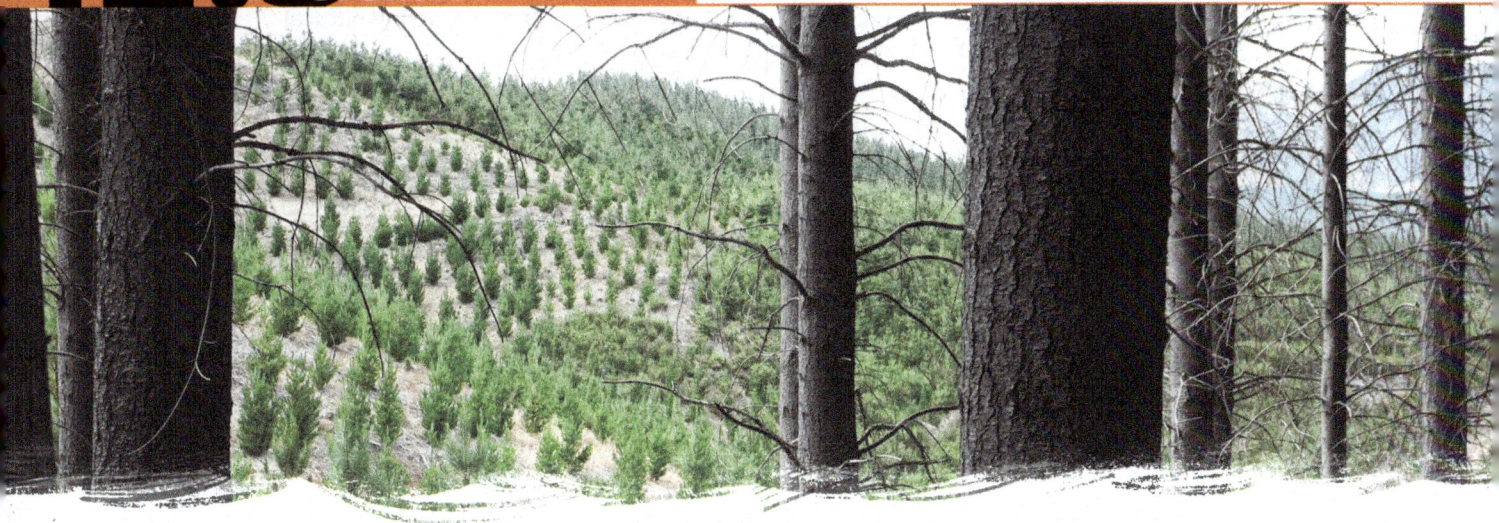

Creation isn't disposable to be thrown away by its consumers, but creation isn't to be worshiped by its users either.

Create a pamphlet on environmental stewardship from a Christian perspective. Use the following questions to guide your categories and content. A main purpose of this pamphlet is to respond biblically to those who want to abuse creation as well as to those who want to idolize creation.

1. **What does the Bible teach about creation in Romans 8:19–23, 2 Peter 3:13, and Revelation 21:1, 5?**

   Creation will be redeemed when it is restored to its former state. God doesn't intend to scrap His very good creation; rather, He will make all creation new again, as well as redeem and restore the bodies of His children. Creation is not a disposable resource; it endures into the eternal state and is eternally important to the Creator.

2. **What is foolish about the actions of those described in Romans 1:23–25?**

   They pursued the worship of mortal created things instead of worshiping the immortal Creator.

3. **What does creation point to in Psalm 19:1–4? How does this truth protect against any notion of idolizing or worshiping creation?**

   God is glorious and has universally demonstrated His great creative abilities into His creation. The Creator is greater than the creation, so He is the only one who should be worshiped and praised.

4. **What should be our responses to God as creator of a beautiful and sustaining world?**

   We should worship Him through gratitude, thankfulness, careful stewardship, and prudent planning for both ongoing and long-term use of the earth and its resources.

5. **How should you respond to someone who endorses littering freely, wasting natural resources, and refusing to reuse or repurpose usable items?**

A biblical worldview demands that we apply what the Bible teaches to how we see the world and live our lives. Being

wasteful is irresponsible. There is no virtue in irresponsibility or wastefulness. In God's wisdom, He gave us

this world, so it pleases Him when His creation is used and maintained with respect and order. To disorder or misuse

what He has so graciously given us is a gross mishandling of creation. The bigger picture must be kept in mind. One

wrapper tossed on the ground, a few gallons of wasted water, and one fixable item in the garbage won't upset the

earth's order as we know it. But each of these small incidences comes from a biblical worldview that is lacking in this

area of study and necessary stewardship.

6. **How should you respond to someone who elevates caring for the planet to a level that is on par with idolizing it?**

It is secular and unbiblical to view the planet as a savior or divine life-giver. Even though people and societies can

make poor decisions and cause great harm to the environment, God is sovereign and oversees all things. This doesn't

get humanity off the hook, but responsible stewardship of the earth isn't the same as worshiping it. It involves

developing a careful and thorough plan for responsible and faithful actions that don't restrict humanity's

livelihood and flourishing. This requires using God's gifts of plants, animals, and natural resources rather than

leaving them entirely undisturbed.

13.1 When Faced with Divorce

Answer the questions below.

1. **What would be an unbiblical, judgmental response to someone going through a divorce? What would be the better response?**

   Examples of unbiblical responses include assuming that someone in the marriage was unfaithful or assuming that the divorce does not align with the biblical allowances for divorce. A better response would include remaining silent until you have heard the whole matter and determining whether or not you are an appropriate person to biblically help in the situation.

2. **What would be an inappropriate response—even if what you say is biblical—if your relationship is not a position of authority or closeness to that person? What would be the appropriate response to someone you are not close to?**

   An example of an unbiblical response would be trying to figure out more than you need to know or more than people are willing to share. An appropriate response would be to assure that person that you will be praying for them both.

3. **What would be an appropriate, compassionate response to innocent people directly affected by the decisions of others?**

   An appropriate response would be to communicate how you share in their sorrow and how you desire to be an encouraging friend in their hardship.

4. **How could distancing yourself from people involved in a divorce or keeping silent about a divorce be unbiblical and hurtful?**

   Staying silent and distant could communicate a lack of love toward the people involved in the divorce.

5. **Who should you go to for counsel on how to respond biblically to friends or family going through a divorce?**

   You could talk to a pastor, a Bible teacher, a parent, or another godly adult.

Identify what verses in Proverbs 7 teach each of these principles.

_____7_____ **1.** Don't naïvely think you are above sin and its consequences. Stay on guard.

_____8–9, 12_____ **2.** Don't put yourself in compromising situations.

_____10_____ **3.** Don't approve of or practice immodesty; both men and women can be culpable of either enticing or lusting due to immodest conduct or something immodestly worn.

__10–11, 16–18, 21__ **4.** Don't approve of or practice dirty or impure communication, be it veiled or obvious.

_____13_____ **5.** Don't play around with physical intimacy that draws you into sinful physical intimacy.

_____13–21_____ **6.** Don't be duped by flattery and enticement to sin.

_____19–20_____ **7.** Don't be alone without accountability with someone you might be tempted into sexual sin with; welcome the oversight of others who will help protect you.

_____22–27_____ **8.** Count the ruinous cost of immorality.

For four of the principles above, provide a specific scenario from your life where it would apply. For each scenario, describe a biblical response, identify how the scenario could lead to ethical compromise, and describe how to biblically seek forgiveness after compromising.

How would you respond to the following scenarios? Be sure to include one or two Scripture passages in your response.

Students should be paired for this activity.

SCENARIO 1

A friend confides in you that she has been struggling with same-sex attraction. She is convinced that it would be wrong to embrace homosexual behavior, but the feelings are just who she is. So, she has decided to embrace both her identity as a lesbian and her identity as a Christian.

SCENARIO 2

A friend reveals to you that he has been reading articles from Christians who argue that the Bible doesn't condemn committed homosexual relationships. He explains how freeing it is to know these desires are natural and have been part of him since childhood, especially since he has been burdened with overwhelming feelings of guilt. Now your friend is convinced that what he feels is natural, normal, and good, and that it does not violate the Bible.

SCENARIO 3

A family member comes out as lesbian and rejects the biblical Christianity that she grew up in. She is not hateful toward you and your family regarding your Christianity, and she still wants to be involved in family activities.

SCENARIO 4

A family member comes out as gay and rejects the biblical Christianity that he grew up in. He is hateful toward you and your family regarding your Christianity, and he wants nothing to do with your family and its get-togethers.

SCENARIO 5

You're excited to start your first job. Part of your training involves watching videos on diversity, including diverse sexual identities, and signing your commitment to embrace such diversity in the workplace.

SCENARIO 6

It's your first opportunity to vote in a national election. Both presidential candidates have records of supporting homosexuality and transgenderism, and both promise further support as president (even though the party of one has historically not supported LGBTQ+ causes).

SCENARIO 7

It's Pride Month, and many social media accounts are posting rainbow symbols to celebrate. Someone at work accuses you of homophobia unless you symbolize your support.

Select a number of factors from Section 13.4 in your textbook that could be involved when a couple is struggling to have children. List the ways that you could offer counsel in this situation, then create a short and simple video of the counsel you would offer to your future self, your future spouse, or a loved one. You may use your list to create a script if it would be helpful.

Students should create a video that reflects what they learned in Section 13.4.

prayer journal

Prayer Journal 1.1

Read Exodus 34:6. Pray through each of God's attributes mentioned in this verse. Thank God for His mercy, grace, patience, love, and faithfulness. Tell the Lord specific ways each of these attributes have impacted you and why you are grateful for His faultless character and sovereign provision.

Prayer Journal 1.2

Read Genesis 1:31 and Proverbs 3:19–20. Pray that God would show you how to appreciate the good ways He has arranged and organized His universe. Pray that He would open your eyes to the creational norms underlying all aspects of life, even in the broken state the Fall has left the world in. Pray that God would give you grace to embrace and pursue God's good purposes for His creation, even though you might suffer pushback or persecution.

Prayer Journal 1.3

Read Genesis 1:26 30. Pray that God will give you a renewed sense of the dignity and value that each person (man and woman; young and old; rich and poor; any ethnicity) has as an image-bearer of God. Pray that God would give you grace to fulfill the Creation Mandate and that you would be a faithful steward who gives Him glory in all your endeavors.

Prayer Journal 2.1

Read Proverbs 2:6, Job 28:28, and James 1:5. After recognizing the great effects of the Fall on the created order and on the human nature, you should be driven to your knees in dependence on God's grace to help you grapple with the ethical difficulties and the ethical choices that you're faced with in this life. If you seek wisdom from the Lord, He will guide you to rightly apply His Word to your life. Write out a prayer that reflects your heart's desires in relation to the truths found in these verses (and their contexts if need be).

Prayer Journal 2.2

Read Psalm 119:104, 128 and Colossians 2:8. False ways can seem very appealing, yet they are deceptive. Therefore, they should be despised and turned from.Write out a prayer that reflects your heart's desires in relation to the truths found in these verses.

Prayer Journal 2.3

Read 2 Peter 1:3 and Psalm 25:4; 119:15, 48. God's Word provides the sufficient guidance we need to make judgments as we seek to wisely evaluate all things. We need to know His precepts above all else.Write out a prayer that reflects your heart's desires in relation to the truths found in these verses.

Prayer Journal 3.1

Read Ezekiel 36:27. Begin with thanking God for fulfilling His New Covenant promise of the Spirit. Ask for the Spirit's help in recognizing areas of your life that need to be brought into alignment with God's law. Pray for grace to walk in God's statutes. Thank Him for hearing your prayer for Christ's sake. Then step out in faith, believing that God will cause you to walk in His statues as He promised.

Prayer Journal 3.2

Read Proverbs 9:10. Begin with praising God for His infinite wisdom and for being the source of all true wisdom. Confess ways that you have chosen the wisdom of the world over the wisdom of God. Since wisdom begins with a proper recognition of who God is, pray for a greater awareness of God's awesome greatness and power over all creation. Ask for wisdom to make choices in keeping with creational norms for God's glory.

Prayer Journal 3.3

Read Deuteronomy 28:47–48. Pray for grace to recognize how serious joyless service is to God. Ask God for eyes to see the connection between serving God with joy and glorifying God in your service. Confess those times that you have served Him without gladness and ask Christ for forgiveness. Pray that God would satisfy your heart with Himself so that you might serve Him with gladness. Thank Him for His willingness to help you grow in this area as one of His redeemed children.

Prayer Journal 4.1

Read Philippians 4:8. Pray that the inputs into your life would be characterized by all that is listed in this verse. If you have been partaking in a regular diet of things that do not match what is described here, then pray that you would rely on the Holy Spirit to fight the sin in your life and put it off. Pray that you would replace it with that which is excellent or virtuous.

Prayer Journal 4.2

Read Proverbs 4:20–27. Pray that you would be diligent to guard your heart. Everything else in your life flows out from what's in your heart. Pray that you would rightly ponder your path so that you would be established in the right way. Pray that you would remain on the right path rather than swerving into evil.

Prayer Journal 5.1

Read Hebrews 11:6. Begin with praising God for the joy of approaching Him through faith in Christ. Confess ways that doubting God and His Word has negatively impacted your ethical choices. Ask for grace to trust God's Word when the world's lies are pulling you in the opposite direction. Pray for help to make choices that please God, even when those choices look foolish to the world. Thank God for giving you courage to live by faith in a doubting world.

Prayer Journal 5.2

Read 1 John 3:18. Begin with thanking God for His love, especially for demonstrating His love in the gift of His Son. Admit your dependency on God for the ability to love Him and to love others. Pray for help to lovingly apply God's law and creational norms in the various relationships that you have. Ask for wisdom to discern ways that the world abuses love and pray that you would remain faithful to God's definition of love.

Prayer Journal 5.3

Read Romans 15:13. Begin with praising God for being the God of Hope. Bring to God any fears and discouragements you may be experiencing, knowing there is no shame for those who are in Christ Jesus as they approach their Father above. Ask God to fill you with joy and peace through belief in His promises. Pray for help to keep your hope grounded in God's character and promises, and not in the changing circumstances of this life.

Prayer Journal 6.1

Read Psalm 71:19 and 2 Thessalonians 1:11. Thank God for His perfect righteousness and abundant goodness. Realize that praising God for His righteousness means submitting to Him as the Judge of your own sinfulness. Praise God for His goodness in sending Christ to redeem sinful humanity.

Prayer Journal 6.2

Read Proverbs 4:5–11. Pray that the Lord would give you wisdom and understanding through Scripture, godly influences, and His faithfulness in your experiences. He will help you know what to do and when to do it. Ask the Lord for prudence during challenging times and hard decisions. God's wisdom and the understanding He gives are key to practicing the virtue of prudence.

Prayer Journal 6.3

Read Ephesians 6:10–11, 13, Philippians 3:13–14, and Colossians 3:23. Pray that God would give you the strength to be diligent, the patience to stay faithful, and the boldness to be courageous in every aspect of your life. All three virtues are necessary and cannot be pursued one at a time. Ask God to prepare you for scenarios in your life where you will need to use each of these virtues.

Prayer Journal 6.4

Read 1 Corinthians 9:25–27 and 2 Thessalonians 2:4. Pray that God would show you areas of your life where you lack self-control. Pray that God would give you the diligence to pursue temperance in your character. Ask God to give you patience in the big things and in the little things of life.

Prayer Journal 7.1

Read Matthew 12:18–21. Pray that God would conform you into Christ's image by showing you how to imitate His humility, meekness, and gentleness. Pray that God would open your eyes to your own pride, anger, and harshness. Ask for the Spirit to guide you toward humility where you have been proud, meekness where you have often displayed anger, and gentleness where you have been harsh.

Prayer Journal 7.2

Read Romans 2:4. God's kindness and compassion to sinners undeserving of grace or mercy is the main motivator for you to show kindness and compassion to others. You don't have to be a "nice person" to practice kindness and compassion. Pray for a heart that expresses these virtues when you interact with all people, especially those who have needs you can meet.

Prayer Journal 7.3

Read Philippians 4:4–7. Pray that the Lord will help you grow in gratitude, joy, and peace. Ask Him to rid you of anxiety as you seek to rejoice in God's sovereignty over your life. Thank God for the peace He gives that allows you to have a closer and sweeter communion with your Savior. Pray that God will use your practice of these virtues to have an impact on your friends and family as they interact with you.

Prayer Journal 7.4

Read Hebrews 6:17–18. Pray that God would open your eyes to see the areas of your life where small, white, or well-meaning lies have become commonplace. One of the many reasons God is a refuge is because He is trustworthy—He won't and He can't lie. God's faithfulness to being truthful indicates the importance of truth telling. Ask God to help you continually realize that lying and falsehood are products of the Devil's doing.

Prayer Journal 8.1

Read Ephesians 5:10. Make this passage (and its context) a key prayer for your life throughout the year as you seek to make ethical applications in all of life. Write out three specific areas that you would like the Lord to help you to rightly discern how to make ethical decisions.

Prayer Journal 8.2

Read 2 Peter 1:3. You can be confident that God has equipped you and provided for you all that you need to make ethical decisions. It comes through a knowledge of Him. Pray that you would pursue glory and virtue by a dedicated pursuit of a knowledge of God and His Word.

Prayer Journal 9.1

Read Psalm 104:29–30. God is sovereign over life and death—even when a tragedy occurs due to the unethical behavior of others. Therefore, even in the face of tragedy, we can rest under the sovereign plan of God in our lives. That does not remove the sorrow from that tragedy, and it does not justify wrongdoing; the wrongdoing most assuredly will be dealt with by God's judgment in due time. We need not question God's goodness or sovereignty. We can turn to the Lord in prayer by submitting to His providence, seeking His comfort, and appealing for His justice as we await the fulfillment of all things. Consider if you or anyone you know has been affected by premature death, then pray for God's solace to be present in that case.

Prayer Journal 9.2

Read Psalm 139:17–18. You can be assured that God is always mindful of every minute detail of your life. This psalm makes it clear that He cares for you and is always there for you. If you find yourself edging toward despair, then you need renewed hope. Biblical hope is a confident expectation in the fulfillment of God's promises. Biblical hope is a confident expectation because it is grounded in a trustworthy, all-powerful person. What has He really promised in this fallen world in life under the sun? But rest assured that He has promised to give you sufficient grace no matter what you face now. He has promised to make all things right in the end. Pray with confidence that you would live in light of this hope.

Prayer Journal 9.3

Read Psalm 127:3–5. This psalm emphasizes that children are a great gift from God. The psalm explains that one of the blessed purposes of children could be to extend the efforts of parents to triumph in their endeavors against the wicked. Children can complete the unfinished work of their parents. Children reside at the center of their parents' happiness. Pray that you would have a biblical attitude toward children as God's blessing to extend your own life's mission rather than viewing children as a nuisance or obstacle to your own self-made dreams.

Prayer Journal 10.1

Read Genesis 9:6. Pray for your local, state, and national leaders and lawmakers. God's Word is clear that capital punishment is just, and a society that follows God's design is blessed by God. Praise God for making you and every human being in His image. Recognize that we have a responsibility to protect each image-bearer of God. Part of how we can do that is to support the death penalty in our states and countries. Pray for your government officials to do just that.

Prayer Journal 10.2

Read Romans 12:18–19. Pray that God will remove any vengeful desires from your heart. You might be vindictive or enjoy getting back at someone, even if it is in some "small" or "harmless" way. Just wars are a measured and appropriate response that isn't vindictive nor a taking of justice into one's own hand, and therefore out of God's hands. God has established war as a means He uses to punish evildoers and defend the innocent. Guard your own heart and motives.

Prayer Journal 10.3

Read Zechariah 7:9–10. Pray that the Lord would give you a heart of kindness and compassion for those in need. Immigrants are often in that category, regardless of their visa status. Pray for your government officials who constantly wrestle with the best approach for handling immigration and its impact on the country.

Prayer Journal 10.4

Read 1 Peter 2:13–14. Pray that the Lord would give you a heart of obedience and submission to your government and its laws. At the same time, ask God to help you see where the government has overstepped its authority and is creating evil laws or mandating evil requirements for its citizens. The government is used by God to punish those who do evil, but God doesn't expect you to obey a government that is requiring you to do evil. Ask God for prudence and courage.

Prayer Journal 11.1

Read Acts 17:26. Begin by praising God for His wisdom in uniting all humanity through a common ancestor in Adam. Acknowledge that all people are equally valuable and worthy of respect because they are in the image of God. If you have any unconfessed sin of racial prejudice or discrimination, ask God for forgiveness (as well as the courage to make amends with the individual, assuming the offense was more than an internal attitude, and that the individual was harmed by your words or actions). Pray for God to give the church wisdom and grace to promote racial harmony in ways that are consistent with the gospel of Jesus Christ.

Prayer Journal 11.2

Read Galatians 5:22–23. Begin by thanking God for the work of the Holy Spirit. Pray that you may grow in the fruit of the Spirit, yielding more and more to His control in your life. Ask for God's help to resist any peer pressure to engage in vices that lead to substance abuse. If you know someone with an addiction, pray for God to replace the addiction with a greater satisfaction in Christ. Pray that God will bring hope to those who are struggling to overcome an addiction.

Prayer Journal 11.3

Read James 3:6–10. Begin by acknowledging to God how unruly the human tongue is, and that it is not right for us to curse people made in His image. Confess any recent misuse of the tongue and turn to Christ for cleansing and renewal. Pray for grace to guard your tongue and for wisdom to speak that which is pleasing to God. Thank God for being patient with you as you grow in the grace and knowledge of Jesus Christ in your communication.

Prayer Journal 11.4

Read 2 Thessalonians 3:10. Begin by asking God to help you view work the way He does. If you view work as a burden, ask for His help to view work as a gift. If you have an entitlement attitude, where you think you should be able to have what you want without working for it, ask God to correct this attitude within you. Pray that God will enable you to use your talents and opportunities to serve others, knowing that it will honor Him and increase your joy in the Lord. Thank God for how He has provided for your physical needs through the employment He has given your parents.

Prayer Journal 12.1

Read Job 1:21 and 12:10. Humbly recognize your place in God's world. Tell Him that you want to submit to His sovereign dealings and plans for your life. The giver of life is also the taker of the same. This recognition doesn't produce fear or anxiety. This truth produces peace and trust in God's good and just ways. Ask God to give you that peace and trust in Him.

Prayer Journal 12.2

Read Matthew 22:39. This commandment is purposefully broad. One of its many applications includes considering and committing to organ donation. Ask God to give you prudence and wisdom and compassion to love others, possibly in this specific way. Pray that God would help you see the value of loving someone at the end of one's life through organ donation.

Prayer Journal 12.3

Read Psalm 104:24, 31. Praise the Lord for His wonderful works in creation. Thank God for His blessing on you as you use what He has made for your survival and enjoyment. Pray that God will teach you to rejoice in His creation as He does. This rejoicing involves caring for creation and demonstrating responsible stewardship.

Prayer Journal 13.1

Read 1 Peter 3:1–7. What character traits do you need to develop to prepare to be a good husband or wife? Pray that the Lord would help you to develop those character traits.

Prayer Journal 13.2

Read Proverbs 1:20–33. What is God's promise if you heed the call of wisdom? Biblical wisdom offers knowledge, wise counsel, and a solemn respect for God and all things He loves. God offers this wisdom to all, but many people instead choose the way of folly—pursuit of their own earthly goals including revelry, pursuit of power and influence, and willful ignorance. This path ultimately leads to destruction and shame. But the way of wisdom is always free to travel, regardless of past mistakes. Pray to the Lord that you would choose the way of wisdom rather than the way of folly.

Prayer Journal 13.3

Read Jude 1. Pray that the Lord would give you a heart to contend for the faith boldly. Have the compassion to pull people out of the fire while keeping yourself unspotted from the world. Pray for the dependence on God required to keep you in the faith.

Prayer Journal 13.4

Read Psalms 127–128. Pray that you would be this kind of blessing to your parents. Pray that you would seek to imprint this mindset on the next generation.

scripture memory

Chapter 1

ROMANS 1:18–20

For the wrath of God is revealed from heaven against all ungodliness and unrighteousness of men, who hold the truth in unrighteousness; Because that which may be known of God is manifest in them; for God hath shewed it unto them. For the invisible things of him from the creation of the world are clearly seen, being understood by the things that are made, even his eternal power and Godhead; so that they are without excuse:

SIGNIFICANCE

God justly punishes evildoers for the sin they commit. This passage reveals that sinful and rebellious humanity suppresses the truth that the creational order displays. Humans have no excuse for sinning against the powerful and divine God by ignoring the creational norms that undergird His world. Believers have the same revelation, but they also have the Scriptures and the Holy Spirit, both of which show and teach God's will for living for Him. May your life align with God's creational norms and biblical revelation for ethical living.

Chapter 2

ROMANS 3:10–12

As it is written, There is none righteous, no, not one: There is none that understandeth, there is none that seeketh after God. They are all gone out of the way, they are together become unprofitable; there is none that doeth good, no, not one.

SIGNIFICANCE

The Bible describes the nature of all human beings. Not even one person could claim self-righteousness. Their sinful depravity affects their understanding (minds). It affects what they seek after (affections). And it causes them to stray from the right path so that they don't do what's good (wills). This condition makes them overall unprofitable (useless or worthless). Such a human condition brings about many ethical difficulties and makes responding to ethical difficulties problematic apart from God's intervening grace.

Chapter 3

If ye then be risen with Christ, seek those things which are above, where Christ sitteth on the right hand of God. Set your affection on things above, not on things on the earth. For ye are dead, and your life is hid with Christ in God. . . .

Put on therefore, as the elect of God, holy and beloved, bowels of mercies, kindness, humbleness of mind, meekness, longsuffering; . . .

SIGNIFICANCE

The Bible sets forth a clear pattern for ethical living that is rooted in the gospel. Colossians 3 begins with the believer's identity in Christ and then proceeds to call him or her to the regular habit of "putting off the old" and "putting on the new." This redemptive strategy for ethical living is unique to Christian ethics. Christians are called to "put on" mercy, kindness, humility, meekness, longsuffering and more. To do this, Christians need constant reminders of who they are in Christ. Many believers tend to forget their identity in Christ and to approach the Christian life with self-willed effort. This only results in discouragement from not being able to measure up. Returning to the biblical pattern is essential. Remember who you are in Christ, then live as one who has been raised with Christ. This approach to ethics follows God's Word and echoes His redemptive power.

Chapter 4

2 PETER 1:3, 5–7

According as his divine power hath given unto us all things that pertain unto life and godliness, through the knowledge of him that hath called us to glory and virtue: . . .

And beside this, giving all diligence, add to your faith virtue; and to virtue knowledge; And to knowledge temperance; and to temperance patience; and to patience godliness; And to godliness brotherly kindness; and to brotherly kindness charity.

SIGNIFICANCE

Every Christian's calling is to live a life characterized by virtue, empowered by the indwelling Holy Spirit. Growing in Christlikeness begins at conversion when a person places faith in Christ. This growth will certainly continue as that person grows in virtue, knowledge, temperance (self-control), patience (perseverance), godliness, brotherly kindness, and charity (love). In fact, 2 Peter 1:9–10 warns that if a professing Christian lacks these characteristics, then that person should check to see whether he or she is truly saved.

Chapter 5

1 CORINTHIANS 13:13

And now abideth faith, hope, charity, these three; but the greatest of these is charity.

SIGNIFICANCE

The Bible gives priority to the virtues of faith, hope, and love because these virtues ensure that all the other virtues remain God-centered. The tendency of many people who study virtues and character building is to treat these things as part of their own self-improvement project. However, the three central virtues guard against this tendency. Faith looks to God for grace and power to grow in all other virtues for the sake of Christ. Hope looks to God's promises for strength to be virtuous in difficult circumstances. Love for people, which includes relating to them in a virtuous manner, depends on an awareness of God's love and loving Him in return. Therefore, to honor God in virtuous living, one must be a believer (faith) who persists in doing good when life is hard (hope) and who is motivated by treasuring God above all (love).

Chapter 6

PHILIPPIANS 4:8

Finally, brethren, whatsoever things are true, whatsoever things are honest, whatsoever things are just, whatsoever things are pure, whatsoever things are lovely, whatsoever things are of good report; if there be any virtue, and if there be any praise, think on these things.

SIGNIFICANCE

Much of ethical decision making—employing virtue developed in believers by the Spirit—has to do with right thinking. Filling one's minds with biblical, moral, and ethical topics and images goes a long way toward making ethical choices that honor the Lord. Christians should be able to identify sinful patterns and topics and, subsequently, stay away from them. Christians are called to prioritize virtue, as well as righteous and good things, to aid their devotion to God and love for others.

Chapter 7

GALATIANS 5:22–23

But the fruit of the Spirit is love, joy, peace, long-suffering, gentleness, goodness, faith, meekness, temperance: against such there is no law.

SIGNIFICANCE

The list of virtues that believers must develop and practice isn't limited to the list in this passage. But this fruit of the Spirit isn't a buffet where you get to pick and choose which ones you want to emphasize in your life. All Christians are called to practice the fruit of the Spirit—all the virtues in this passage and all the virtues found elsewhere in Scripture. Thankfully, believers can always ask the Spirit to help develop this fruit of virtue in their lives. You might, however, get input from those who know you well and concentrate your efforts for a while on a virtue that you lack altogether or hardly ever practice.

Chapter 8

PSALM 119:97, 101–4

O how love I thy law! it is my meditation all the day. . . .

I have refrained my feet from every evil way, that I might keep thy word.

I have not departed from thy judgments: for thou hast taught me.

How sweet are thy words unto my taste! yea, sweeter than honey to my mouth!

Through thy precepts I get understanding: therefore I hate every false way.

SIGNIFICANCE

This passage highlights the law of God, the psalmist's inward motivation of delight in God's law, and his goal to keep God's Word and to remain aligned with God's judgments. All of this leads him to embrace ethical living, hating every false way. By making God's Word his constant meditation and by submitting himself under God's teachings, the psalmist receives the understanding he needs and the transformed character from within to pursue such an ethical lifestyle.

Chapter 9

MATTHEW 5:21–22

Ye have heard that it was said by them of old time, Thou shalt not kill; and whosoever shall kill shall be in danger of the judgment: But I say unto you, That whosoever is angry with his brother without a cause shall be in danger of the judgment: and whosoever shall say to his brother, Raca, shall be in danger of the council: but whosoever shall say, Thou fool, shall be in danger of hell fire.

SIGNIFICANCE

Jesus expounds upon the original meaning of the law with all its implications. At the root of murder is hatred. The sixth commandment's original intent forbade not only murder but also all that underlies murder as well.

Chapter 10

ROMANS 13:1, 4

Let every soul be subject unto the higher powers. For there is no power but of God: the powers that be are ordained of God. . . .

For he is the minister of God to thee for good. But if thou do that which is evil, be afraid; for he beareth not the sword in vain: for he is the minister of God, a revenger to execute wrath upon him that doeth evil.

SIGNIFICANCE

God has ordained that governments have authority in society. But that authority is for the good and flourishing of individuals, families, and other organizations that make up a society. The authority that governments possess comes from God and they, therefore, are responsible to God for how they uphold and defend the good and oppose and punish the bad.

Chapter 11

MATTHEW 7:12

Therefore all things whatsoever ye would that men should do to you, do ye even so to them: for this is the law and the prophets.

SIGNIFICANCE

The Golden Rule is essential for a society to function in an ethical manner. Without it, the bonds of society are easily broken. Therefore, we should pray that Christ will turn our society toward Him so people will treat others as they wish to be treated.

The beauty of the Golden Rule is the simplicity with which it summarizes the law and the prophets. The Golden Rule applies to all of life. Think of the issues discussed in this chapter. How should you respond to a friend who has experienced discrimination? According to the Golden Rule, you should respond to your friend the same way you would desire your friend to treat you under similar circumstances.

How would you respond if an elected official tried to convince you that a state-sponsored lottery could benefit you? You might think of the lives destroyed by gambling and consider how you would feel if people profited from your misery. Similarly, you probably wouldn't post a cruel comment about an enemy on social media if you reflected on what it would be like to be on the receiving end of a cruel posting. Finally, you probably wouldn't steal what others have worked hard to purchase if you thought of someone doing the same to you.

Chapter 12

GENESIS 1:28–30

And God blessed them, and God said unto them, Be fruitful, and multiply, and replenish the earth, and subdue it: and have dominion over the fish of the sea, and over the fowl of the air, and over every living thing that moveth upon the earth. And God said, Behold, I have given you every herb bearing seed, which is upon the face of all the earth, and every tree, in the which is the fruit of a tree yielding seed; to you it shall be for meat. And to every beast of the earth, and to every fowl of the air, and to every thing that creepeth upon the earth, wherein there is life, I have given every green herb for meat: and it was so.

SIGNIFICANCE

This is the latter half of God's Creation Mandate that He gave to Adam and Eve; it is still in effect today. It outlines a large part of humanity's relationship to the earth and its contents. Subduing the earth and having dominion over it impacts scientific research. Someone's view of humanity and the rest of creation is demonstrated through how that person relates to the world. God blesses people by giving them resources and by providing the responsibility to govern creation. A failure to enjoy and responsibly steward those resources and the knowledge they offer is an affront to God.

Chapter 13

1 THESSALONIANS 4:3–5

For this is the will of God, even your sanctification, that ye should abstain from fornication: That every one of you should know how to possess his vessel in sanctification and honour; Not in the lust of concupiscence, even as the Gentiles which know not God:

SIGNIFICANCE

God's commands make clear God's desired will for His people. One of the keys to fulfilling His will for His people's growth in holy living is to turn away from sexual immorality. Every one of God's people should grow in maturity to take responsible control over their own bodily passions so they behave in ways that are set apart from sin—honorable and above reproach. This will be in stark contrast to the surrounding godless culture, driven by lusts for sexually immoral pleasures.